The Magic of a Million

ACTIVITY BOOK

by David M. Schwartz and David J. Whitin

SCHOLASTIC
PROFESSIONAL BOOKS

New York • Toronto • London • Auckland • Sydney

Dedication

To the many teachers who have encouraged their students to explore the endless possibilities of the number 1,000,000— and who have thereby inspired children to find excitement in mathematical discovery. They have our respect, our admiration and our gratitude. Thanks a million!

Teachers may photocopy the designated reproducible pages for classroom use. No other part of this publication may be reproduced in whole or in part, or stored in a retrieval system, or transmitted in any form or by any means, electronic, mechanical, photocopying or otherwise, without written permission of the publisher. For information regarding permission, write to Scholastic Inc., 555 Broadway, New York, NY 10012.

Cover design by Kathy Massaro

Cover art by Chris Murphy

Jacket cover from HOW MUCH IS A MILLION? by David M. Schwartz.
Illustrated by Steven Kellogg. Illustration copyright © 1985 by Steven Kellogg.
By permission of Lothrop, Lee & Shepard Books,
a division of William Morrow & Company, Inc.

Interior illustrations by Michael Moran and Manuel Rivera

Interior photos courtesy David M. Schwartz;
except pages 11 and 17, courtesy David J. Whitin

Interior design by Ellen Matlach Hassell
for Boultinghouse & Boultinghouse, Inc.

Edited by Jean Liccione

ISBN 0-590-70133-9

Copyright © 1998 by David M. Schwartz and David J. Whitin. All rights reserved.

Printed in the USA.

Contents

Introduction

Living in a World of Large Numbers

Children, and a great many adults, love the number 1,000,000. On the surface, it is only a number. But it's a number that motivates and inspires. Early in life, the word *million* becomes an integral part of our vocabulary, even if the number itself remains a somewhat mysterious quantity.

When teachers tap into their students' inherent interest in big numbers—especially 1,000,000, the best-known of them all—they not only answer the oft-heard question, "How much is a million?" They also generate excitement about mathematics in general. And countless classes have found that explor- ing the number 1,000,000 can encompass vir- tually every area of the curriculum, from math and science to reading and social stud- ies. As one child said after participating in activities that involved counting, collecting, calculating, estimating, and measuring vari- ous items in quantities of one million, "A million is more than meets the eye!"

In this book you will see a few of the myr- iad ways that students and teachers together have explored this popular number. Each activity is accompanied by "The Math Classroom in Action," where you will see how some teachers and students investigated one million.

Meet the Authors!

How did you each get involved with the idea of the importance of big numbers?

David Schwartz: As a kid I was interested in math and science. Above all, I liked to think about how to apply math to aspects of daily life in ways that "boggled" my mind. I was fascinated with things that came in large numbers, and things that were large and very distant—like stars. As an adult, these thoughts came back to me as I looked at the stars. How far away are they? How many of them are there? How long would it take for someone to count that high? I thought about how rarely children discover the true mean- ing of the word *awesome*. And from there I moved on to ideas for writing my books about big numbers—*How Much Is a Million?* and *If You Made a Million*.

David Whitin: My interest in large numbers came from reading David Schwartz's books. As my teacher colleagues and I read math/lit- erature books to students, we found these books about one million were extremely appealing to them. From a two-year-old who reported that she had a million mosquito bites, to some eighth grade students who wanted to display a million computer dots, I've discovered that these ideas have a univer- sal appeal. Also, as I work with in-service and pre-service teachers in my university classes, I find that exploring large numbers is a good way for my own students to improve their number sense and gain a better understand- ing of place value.

◀ "999,996, 999,997, 999,998. . ."
That's one long string of popcorn!

◀ What do one million pieces of Cheerios cereal look like? The students in this class tried to find out!

And how did this book come about?

David Whitin: We kept swapping stories about big number projects. With the numerous stories we both had collected about teachers exploring one million in such creative ways, I suggested that we assemble these stories into a resource book for teachers. And that's the book you now are reading!

David Schwartz: Thanks to the creativity, inspiration, and generosity of teachers and students too numerous to list, we collected enough material for a heavyweight tome! What we have here represents a small fraction of the many wonderful activities and projects we have collected. We hope that these activities and snapshots from many math classrooms "in action" will serve as inspiration for more teachers and students to invent their own variations on the "million" theme.

The Magic of a Million and the NCTM Standards

When the National Council of Teachers of Mathematics published their Curriculum and Evaluation Standards for School Mathematics in 1989, they described a direction of change which we have attempted to embody in the activities in this book. The vision of the Standards is "...built around five overall curricular goals for students to achieve: learning to value mathematics, becoming confident in one's own ability, becoming a mathematical problem solver, learning to communicate mathematically, and learning to reason mathematically."

In keeping with the goals of the Standards, we have designed activities that:

★ are conceptually oriented

★ actively involve children in doing mathematics

★ make use of materials including calculators and computers

★ emphasize development of thinking, reasoning, and communication

★ emphasize application of mathematics in purposeful situations

In this book, we've tried to inspire both imagination and mathematical thinking. The investigations are easily adaptable to a range of grade levels. They are an excellent vehicle for helping students reinforce math concepts, record information in an orderly way, and reflect on their processes and thinking through discussion or in a math journal.

◀ Three students' personal takes on David Schwartz's books.

Imagining One Million

Inviting students to imagine one million of something is an appealing way for them to personalize this large number. Whatever the interests of your students—sports, food, television, animals, cars—they can all be tied to one million. Students can have fun drawing some of their "imaginings" to share with the rest of the class. The mathematics comes into play when students are challenged to think of the consequences of their wishes. For example, if you had a million of a particular favorite food, how long would it take to eat it all? Or, if you really did own a million of a particular animal, how much would it cost to feed them all?

IMAGINING INVESTIGATION 1

What Would You Do With a Million?

BIG IDEA: How can we conceptualize one million?

PROCESS SKILLS: recording, problem-formulating, predicting

What to Do

1. Ask students to imagine having a million of something. It's fun to imagine one million of some things—but scary to imagine one million of others! Children usually focus on the desirability of large quantities. But it is worthwhile to see the downside, too. After all, anyone can be entranced by the idea of having one million dollars. But what about one million brothers? As one youngster, perhaps anticipating a busy future, wrote, "Having a million girlfriends could be a problem."

2. Focus a discussion on one million by asking students what they'd like to have one million of. Money will usually come up early in the conversation. What else? Record students' responses on a chart titled "We'd Like a Million _____ But We Wouldn't Want a Million _____".

3. Then copy and distribute Data Sheet 1 on page 63 or Data Sheet 2 on page 64. Note that Data Sheet 2, *Here's What I'd Do With a Million*, contains blank spaces for students' own ideas as well as a list of some starter ideas. You and your students can make your own list of serious and strange things to have. Encourage students to be creative in their responses. Then share results.

Taking It Further

Ask students to look at their lists and speculate about the volume of some of their items. What size container would hold a million jelly beans? How many shelves would hold a million books or a million video games?

The Math Classroom in Action

What Would You Do With a Million?

In Yokayo Elementary School in Ukiah, California, students thought about one million in terms of powers of ten. Each grade level used art projects to show their representations of one, ten, one hundred, one thousand, and so on.

At Washington Avenue Elementary School in Chatham, New Jersey, students thought about one million in another way—what it would be like to spend one million dollars. They delved into magazine ads and catalogs with the challenge of spending exactly one million dollars—down to the penny! Math coordinator Mary Costner supplied students with mock checkbooks and students kept track of their spending. There were some restrictions. For example, students could buy no more than one house, and the house could cost no more than $250,000; they could buy no more than one car, and the car could cost no more than $25,000; students could buy no more than one of any given item. But with a million dollars to spend, a few restrictions were not a problem! The problem was in getting rid of all that money!

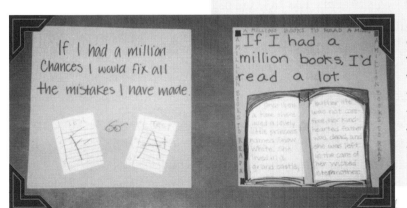

Lisbon Elementary School, in Sacramento, California, took on the challenge of imagining one million, with interesting results. Students wrote about, and illustrated, what they wanted a million of—and what they would do with it. Many adults would probably agree with the sentiments of the student who would "fix all the mistakes I have made"!

IMAGINING INVESTIGATION 2

Explore More!

BIG IDEA: What would we like to investigate involving big numbers?

PROCESS SKILLS: problem posing, problem solving, predicting, verifying, calculating, recording

What to Do

1. Imagining one million of something allows students to see their world through the eyes of a mathematician. With inspiration from David Schwartz's *How Much Is a Million?* invite students to invent their own investigation of a big number (one million or more). They might verify or extend information from *How Much Is a Million?* or they might build an investigation around mathematical wonderings of their own. This is a perfect way to promote real life math—students can investigate problems that affect their own community or that are of particular interest to them.

2. Encourage students to talk with family members, or to use community resources, for ideas and help in calculating if needed. Students might use some of the facts below. Be sure that they describe and justify their work and their reasoning. If you wish, have them use Data Sheet 13 on page 75. (Just change the title at the top of the page before copying.)

Ideas for Big Number Investigations

Recycling and Garbage

★ The glass in a glass bottle lasts one million years.

★ Every year in the United States, 10.6 million tons of glass are discarded, and only 2.6 million tons are recycled.

★ Overall, the U.S. generates 200 million tons of garbage every year.

Animal Facts

★ The heart of a blue-throated hummingbird beats about 1,260 times per minute.

★ A colony of 50 big brown bats eats 123,000 crop-damaging insects in one year.

★ Army ants amass in groups of up to 20 million.

★ It is estimated that 27,950,000 species on earth are insects.

Astronomy Facts

★ The sun is about 93 million miles away from Earth.

★ The Andromeda Galaxy is racing toward the Milky Way Galaxy at 300,000 miles an hour, but the collision won't occur for about 5 billion years.

★ Light travels 186,000 miles per second.

The Math Classroom in Action

Explore More!

In Kathy Reed's combination third/fourth grade class at Sweetbriar Elementary School in Troutdale, Oregon, students built a book, called Big Number Project, around their investigations of big numbers. Kathy encouraged wide-ranging investigations and students wrote about their numerical explorations and illustrated their work. Some of the students came up with mathematical questions that required vast amounts of outside research, including reading and talking to experts, to answer. One student, for example, investigated how many sheets of paper could be made from one log truck's load of logs. Another wondered how many scoops of ice cream it would take to fill the swimming pool of the local community college.

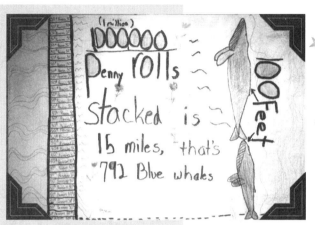

Students had to develop a mathematical strategy for answering their own questions, explain their thinking, and describe any difficulties they had in answering the questions.

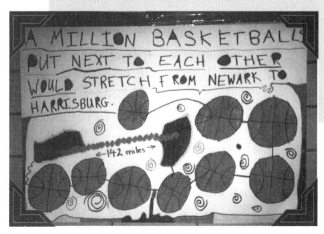

Fourth-grade students at Indian Lane Elementary School in Media, Pennsylvania, did their own research to make "million problems." They presented their calculations in a novel way: each student made a poster with the problem stated, and viewers could lift a flap to find the answer. This project generated a lot of interest throughout the school as everyone walked around reading the questions and lifting the flaps to see the answers.

Sports-minded students are everywhere! At Washington Avenue School, in Chatham, New Jersey, students used information about their favorite sports to do some calculations with big numbers. One student chose to run a line of basketballs from the capital of New Jersey to the capital of neighboring Pennsylvania. A map is part of the poster that illustrates his work.

9

Counting to One Million

When they read in David Schwartz's book *How Much Is a Million?* that it takes 23 days to count to one million, many students refuse to believe it. When they exhibit this skepticism of data, or try to confirm it, they are demonstrating an important attitude in mathematics. Living as they do in an age in which they are inundated with numerical information, students who challenge data become critical consumers of facts and figures. Counting to one million gives students a real reason to use calculators to find averages and calculate different counting rates. So take a deep breath and join the counting fun!

COUNTING INVESTIGATION 1

Clocking One Million

BIG IDEA: How long does it take to count to one million?

PROCESS SKILLS: counting, recording, explaining methods, developing mathematical strategies

What to Do

1. Ask students how long they think it will take to count to one million. If you've read David Schwartz's *How Much Is a Million?* ask students if they think 23 days, as reported in the book, is a reasonable answer.

2. Tell students you will assume that all the numbers between 1 and 1,000,000 take the same amount of time to say. Ask a volunteer to come to the front of the classroom and begin counting. After one minute has passed, write on the chalkboard the number the counter reached. Discuss the results with the class. What conclusions can they reach, with this sample, about counting to one million?

3. Invite students to make some estimates about how long it will take to reach one million, based on this one-minute counting sample. Ask them to suggest ways they could find an answer.

4. Let students try out their suggestions, working in pairs or small groups. If you wish, copy Data Sheet 3 on page 65 and have students use it to record their findings.

5. When all groups are finished, discuss their results. Are all answers within a similar range? If not, ask the class to decide why not. If students do not raise the idea themselves, you might want to point out that as numbers get bigger, they take longer to say. Can students figure out a way to account for this important fact?

The Math Classroom in Action

Clocking One Million

In one fifth-grade class, Philip counted to 194 in two minutes. He calculated his rate of counting: 194 ÷ 120 seconds = 1.6 seconds. Philip reasoned that it takes 1.6 seconds to say each number. He used that data to calculate the time it would take to count to one million. His conclusion (numbers are rounded):

$$1.6 \times 1,000,000 = 1,600,000 \text{ seconds}$$
$$1,600,000 \div 60 = 26,667 \text{ minutes}$$
$$26,667 \div 60 = 444 \text{ hours}$$
$$444 \div 24 = 19 \text{ days}$$

This would be a good solution to the problem if it took the same amount of time to count all the numbers. Although it does not, students often use this as an assumption.

Some fourth graders realized that larger numbers take longer to say than smaller ones. They decided to have different children start counting at different numbers. Then they counted for one minute and recorded their results in a chart. With their teacher's help, they used a calculator to see how far each person would have gotten in an hour (multiply by 60) and in a day (multiply that result by 24), if they continued at that same rate.

Some of the students' insights into factors affecting the counting time are:

★ Larger numbers take longer to say.

★ Some people count more quickly than others.

★ If you tried to just keep counting to reach one million, you would have to take breaks and it would take longer than the calculated time.

COUNTING INVESTIGATION 2

Double-Time

BIG IDEA: How does skip-counting change the time it takes to count to one million?

PROCESS SKILLS: counting by numbers other than 1, making predictions, recording, comparing results

What to Do

1. Ask students if they can think of some faster ways to count to one million. Some students will likely suggest trying to say numbers faster. Others will probably suggest skip-counting by 2s, 5s, 10s, 100s, or 1,000s. If a variety of numbers is suggested, ask children to predict which will be the fastest and why they think so. How much faster would it be than counting by 1s?

2. Divide the class into small groups. Give each group a number to count by, and challenge each group to figure out how long it will take to count to one million.

3. If you wish, copy and distribute Data Sheet 4 on page 66 and have students use it as they work. When all groups are finished, compile the results in a class chart such as the one shown below.

Number Counted By	Time It Takes to Reach One Million

Taking It Further

★ Ask students how they would figure out the number of tricycles it would take to have one million tricycle wheels. Could this question be answered by skip-counting? How about the number of octopuses to have one million octopus legs? Or soccer teams to have a million players?

★ Challenge students to look for patterns when they count. Is counting by 10s twice as fast as counting by 5s? Is counting by 8s four times as fast as counting by 2s? How many numbers would be counted if you counted to 1,000,000 by 2s, 3s, 7s, etc.? Ask students how they could figure that out.

Double-Time

After their class had read David Schwartz's *How Much Is a Million?*, students at Laurel Wood Elementary School in Salinas, California, were inspired to investigate the size of bowl that would be needed to hold one million goldfish. What could be more natural than to use "real" goldfish! These students employed the idea of skip counting using a BIG number. As they bagged groups of 200 fish, they found that they needed 5,000 bags to count one million goldfish.

Some fourth grade students were interested in figuring out how long it would take to count to one million using a number greater than 1. The class figured that if they counted by 2s they should reach one million in half the time, or 11.5 days. When their teacher asked them how long it would take them to count to one million by 5s, Ben reasoned, "Well, it has to be less than 5 days because 5 times 5 is 25, and it's only 23 days. It must be between 4 and 5 days." Students used calculators and compiled this chart:

Counting by	Time to Reach One Million
1s	23 days
2s	11.5 days
3s	7.6666 days
4s	5.75 days
5s	4.6 days
6s	3.8333 days
7s	3.2857 days
8s	2.875 days
9s	2.5555 days
10s	2.3 days

One student looked at the sequence of numbers 1, 2, 4, 8, and 16, and found that each time a number is doubled, the amount of time to reach one million is cut in half. The moral of this investigation: If you want to finish a job in a hurry, work twice as fast and you'll be done in half the time!

COUNTING INVESTIGATION 3

Say it or Write It?

BIG IDEA: Is it faster to count aloud to one million or to write numbers from one to one million?

PROCESS SKILLS: counting, recording, finding an average, explaining methods

What to Do

1. Ask students which they think would take longer: to count aloud from one to one million or to write numbers from one to one million. As students respond, ask them to give reasons for their answers. Then invite them to try it out.

2. Have ten students write for one minute. Record the number each student reaches. It is likely that students will not all reach the same number after a minute of writing. This is a perfect time to introduce or reinforce the concept of averaging to determine a number that can be used as a benchmark. Show students how to add the 10 numbers and then divide the sum by 10 to find the average.

3. If you wish, copy and distribute Data Sheet 5 on page 67. Suggest that students use their benchmark number as the starting point. Then ask students to figure out how long it would take to reach one million by writing the numbers. They should use any method they like to accomplish this, including using a calculator. Remind students to complete the portions of the recording sheet that ask them to explain and evaluate their procedures.

4. When everyone is finished, ask students to share their results. As different students present their findings, have them explain the methods they used. If results vary, ask students to discuss why this might happen. If two students have used the same method, do their answers agree? If not, whose answer is correct?

978,625 978,626 978,627 978,628 978,629 978,630 978,631 978,632 978,333 978,634

BIG Number Fact

There are about 100 billion stars in the Milky Way galaxy. If you tried to count to 100 billion, it could take as long as 15,000 years.

978,640 978,641 978,642 978,643 978,644 978,645 978,646 978,647 978,648 978,649

The Math Classroom in Action

Say It or Write It?

When some sixth graders wanted to know if it would be faster to count or write to one million, one student suggested that they should start by having everyone write as fast as they could for one minute and see how far they got. The class agreed, and wrote furiously for one minute. Their ending numbers ranged from 41 to 67.

The students decided to add all the figures and divide by the number of students to find the average. They determined the average to be 53.

However, they decided that larger numbers would take longer to write than smaller numbers. They wanted to take that fact into account in their calculations. Instead of conducting additional tests for the larger numbers, which they could have done, they decided to estimate some of the other rates. They agreed on the following rates:

1- and 2-digit numbers	53 per minute
3-digit numbers	35 per minute
4-digit numbers	27 per minute
5-digit numbers	21 per minute
6-digit numbers	18 per minute
7-digit numbers	only one number would have to be written.

The students then added up these rates and divided by 5, rounding off their answer to get an average rate.

$$53 + 35 + 27 + 21 + 18 + 1 = 155 \qquad 155 \div 5 = 30$$

The students then calculated the time in the following manner:

$30 \times 60 \text{ minutes} = 1,800$ (the number reached in one hour)
$1,800 \times 24 = 43,200$ (the number reached in one day)
$1,000,000 \div 43,200 = 23$ (the number of days to reach 1,000,000)

Some interesting strategizing went into this solution, but unfortunately it is mathematically flawed. Ninety percent of the numbers between 1 and 1,000,000 are 6-digit numbers, but averaging the various rates gives equal weight to all of them. It would have been reasonable to use the 6-digit figure of 18 and throw the others away. Or students could have raised the figure a bit—perhaps to 19 or 20 per minute—to account for how much faster one can say the numbers between 1 and 100,000. The students in this class were amazed that their final answer matched the figure in *How Much Is a Million?* We think it's amazing, too, but we believe the close coincidence of the two figures is just that—a coincidence!

973,065 973,066 973,067 973,068 973,069 973,070 973,071 973,072 973,073 973,074 973,075 973,076 973,077 973,078 973,079 973,080 973,081 973,082 973,083 973,084 973,085 973,086 973,087 973,088 973,089 973,090 973,091

COUNTING INVESTIGATION 4

Faster Than a Speeding Calculator!

BIG IDEA: Is counting with a calculator faster than counting aloud?

PROCESS SKILLS: using a calculator, recording, explaining methods

What to Do

1. Invite students to suggest ways they could use a calculator to help them count to one million. Many creative suggestions will emerge. But if you want to stress strictly counting, you may need to demonstrate how to count with a calculator—by pressing 1 + 1 and then pressing "equals" again and again. Show students what the calculator records when you do this. If each student or small groups have calculators, invite them to try.

2. Ask a volunteer to use a calculator and to begin counting. After a minute, stop and record the result on the chalkboard. Compare the result with students' results when they counted aloud for one minute. Discuss with students: We know that numbers take longer to say as they get larger. But does it take longer to compute in this way on the calculator as the numbers get larger? Why or why not?

3. Invite students to predict how long it will take to reach one million using the calculator. If only one calculator is available, you can complete the activity as a class and compile the results together.

4. Discuss the results. Ask children to talk about what they discovered as advantages or disadvantages of using a calculator to do the counting. Was it more tiring to say numbers or punch calculator buttons? Was it more likely that you would lose track of counting by one method or the other? Ask students if they can think of any practical reason to use a calculator in this way to count to one million. (We can't!)

Taking It Further

★ Students might like to try setting up a computer program to count to one million. They can then compare that rate to the results of counting with a calculator. They might program the computer to count by 2s, 3s, 4s, and so on and again compare the results. You can also show students how they can use a calculator to count by 2s, 3s, or any number.

★ With your class, discuss the question: Is it ever necessary to count to one million? If so, when? How would you do it?

The Math Classroom in Action

Faster Than a Speeding Calculator!

Jordan and Adam decided to use the speed of a calculator to help them reach the one million mark in record time. Here's what Adam wrote about their procedures:

"Jordan and I took a calculator and pressed 1 + 1 and then kept pressing 'equals'. We timed it with a stopwatch. We would switch off. We reached 18,311 in 1 hour, 5 minutes and 57 seconds. We then figured that it would take 54.5 more hours. It would take 55.5 hours to get to 1,000,000 on a calculator."

(Although they didn't need to, since they were using a calculator, the boys decided to round their total to 18,000 and then divide 1,000,000 by that number to get 55.5 hours.)

Fourth grader Casey used the calculator to figure out how long it would take to count to one million by 2s, 3s, 4s, and so on. When she reached 11s, she found that it would take 2.0909 days. This led to a conversation with her teacher about rounding, since she wasn't sure how to round that number to the nearest tenth.

The calculator + curiosity + teacher's help = new learning for Casey!

COUNTING INVESTIGATION 5

Getting There in a Hurry

BIG IDEA: How long does it take to reach one million using doubling?

PROCESS SKILLS: counting, doubling and other geometric progressions, recording, explaining results

What to Do

1. Invite students to try doubling numbers. Work together at first, so they get an idea of how quickly doubling "adds up." For example:

   Start with 1. Double it. We get (2).
   Start with 2. Double it. We get (4).
   Start with 4. Double it. We get (8).
   Start with 8. Double it. We get (16).
   Start with 16. Double it. We get (32).

   Ask students to predict how many doublings it would take to reach 1,000,000. Record their guesses. Have students work in pairs or small groups to find out. They will undoubtedly be amazed to see that they'll reach 1,048,576 on the twentieth double.

2. Introduce the concept (not necessarily the term) of a geometric progression: multiplying by a certain constant each time; in this case, by 2. Give some real-life examples of geometric progressions and have students discover the implications. For example *The population of Nicaragua is about 4.5 million people. It will double every 20 years. In a lifetime of 60 years, what will happen to the population?*

   Present time . . . 4.5 million people
   In 20 years. . . . . (9 million)
   In 40 years. . . . . (18 million)
   In 60 years. . . . . (36 million)

   Using an almanac or other source of population statistics, have students determine population growths of various countries. Discuss the problems of this kind of growth.

3. Doubling amounts of money is always fun. Copy and distribute Data Sheet 6 on page 68 and have students complete it to see how long it would take to become a millionaire using a doubling payment schedule.

Taking It Further

★ What happens when you triple your way toward one million? Challenge students to find out. If larger numbers produce more rapid expansion toward one million, ask students to investigate doubling numbers less than one, such as ½ or ¼.

★ Bacteria are single-celled organisms that reproduce by dividing in two. Suppose a certain kind of bacterium divides every 30 minutes. How long would it take before a single bacterial cell has become 1,000,000 bacteria?

The Math Classroom in Action

Getting There in a Hurry

One group of fifth graders attempted to "trick" some unsuspecting parents into the double-a-penny-each-day method of paying allowance. Some students even wrote official contracts for their parents to sign. Here are the results they reported:

"When we walked into the house I ran to get the contract. When I gave it to my mom she was just about to sign when my dad had to figure it out. I was frantically trying to wave him off. . . But it still didn't work. But wait—one more chance left—do your 'Sorry face'! Then my mom yells, 'Quit pouting!' Oh well. Don't ever try to bribe your parents because sooner or later they're going to say those two letters—NO!" —*Matt*

"I was thinking about what my dad would say. I thought he would say no. I wrote an interesting contract to try to get him in a good mood. Then I went to him and said, 'Hey Dad, you know, instead of paying me $3.75 for my allowance, pay me $.25 and double it each day for only two weeks.' And he said, 'Forget it. Do you know how much money that is?' I said, 'Yes sir.' And he pulled out a calculator and figured it out and was astonished." —*Tara*

"I approached my dad after we were done eating supper [and asked him about a doubling payment for my allowance]. He said, 'I guess I will.' Then I showed him how much money he would have to pay me. Then he said, 'There goes my tax money!'" —*Brian*

Collecting One Million

There is perhaps no better way to experience the magnitude of one million than by attempting to collect one million of something. A collection project gives children a chance to see, perhaps for the only time in their lives, a pile of one million objects. But it does much more—it generates excitement about big numbers, and it teaches a great deal about our number system. Since collecting one million objects usually takes some time, students gain a patient understanding for how large this number is. As the collection grows, students see first-hand the emerging pattern of hundreds, thousands, ten thousands. Graphing the results of the growing collection is a way for students to examine their efforts. The data from the graph encourages them to predict and verify the amount of time needed to reach their goal.

COLLECTING INVESTIGATION 1

A Hill of Beans

BIG IDEA: How can we keep track of one million things?

PROCESS SKILLS: counting, collecting, recording, explaining methods

What to Do

1. Ask students to suggest items they might gather to make a collection of one million. Don't steer possibilities at first; rather, encourage students to brainstorm a list. Write all the suggestions on the chalkboard. Then review the list with the class, and ask students to evaluate the practicality of each collection. The field of possibilities is vast, but the best choices are inexpensive or free, small, and light. Dry beans work nicely.

2. When students have narrowed the list to three or four possibilities, ask them to vote on what the class will actually collect. If your whole school will be involved, the list and voting could be done by posting one suggestion per class and having everyone vote. Volunteers can record and tally the votes.

3. Be sure students discuss where materials will be stored as they are collected. They also might want to consider what could be done with the materials, if anything, when the collection is complete.

4. An important task in the collection of one million is determining how counting will be tracked and in what quantities the collected materials should be stored. You might make envelopes of 100 beans each; jars of 1,000 beans; and so on. Use Data Sheet 7 on page 69, if you wish.

The Math Classroom in Action

A Hill of Beans

The children of Julius Marks Elementary School in Lexington, Kentucky, created an enormous hill of beans—one million altogether—that they planned to donate to a local food pantry. But the food handlers had to turn them down since the food had been handled. The experience inspired new lyrics to an old song.

(Sing to the tune of "I've Been Working on the Railroad.")

We've been counting navy beans, for a solid week!
If we see another bean, we will all scream, "Eeek!"
Yes, we think we have a million, but they weigh a ton!
Yes, we counted to a million, thank God we are done!
Gotta million beans, gotta million beans,
Gotta million beans, we know oh, oh, oh.
Gotta million beans, gotta million beans,
Gotta million beans, Yo Ho!

At Armstrong Elementary School in Dallas, Texas, the classes of Debbie Rhines and Jan Norris jointly undertook "Project One Million." By turning their classrooms into "factories" for processing computer holes, children achieved an impressive collection of exactly one million and also deepened their understanding of our number system.

Rhines and Norris used the perforated edges of computer paper, dotted with holes. They cut the perforated strips into two pieces, of ten holes apiece, and discarded the remaining piece with two holes. Working in groups of four, children formed "factories" that stapled ten 10-strips together into one 100-stack, rubber banded ten 100-stacks into one 1,000-bundle, and bagged ten 1,000-bundles together into one 10,000-bag.

At times, children tried working alone to see how their production would compare with that of the group. They were able to assess the advantages and disadvantages of job specialization. As Claire discovered when she worked apart from her team, "They made a lot more because they could work together and I couldn't. Also, if you're doing the same thing over and over again, it's more boring but it's a lot faster once you get good at it."

Fifth grade teachers Leasha Segars and Lindy Hopkins, at Saltillo Elementary School in Saltillo, Mississippi, embarked on a collection project using popped kernels of corn. The project took six weeks. One big challenge was where to store a million pieces of popcorn. The father of one of the students solved the problem with the loan of a cotton wagon—20 feet long, 7 feet wide, and 6 feet high. The wagon was parked behind the school, and every day students added more popcorn, eventually filling it with one million pieces of popcorn to a depth of two feet. And in the end, pigs at a local pig farm had a delicious treat as students solved the final problem of how to use one million pieces of popcorn!

COLLECTING INVESTIGATION 2

Making It Pay

BIG IDEA: How can we collect and keep track of a million pennies? How many dollars is that?

PROCESS SKILLS: counting, recording, calculating

What to Do

1. Ask students to imagine what a million pennies might look like. Would they fill your classroom wastebasket? The classroom itself? The entire school? Students tend to overestimate the volume occupied by a million objects, and they may be surprised once they have refined their guesses. With a small sample, such as a jar filled with one hundred pennies, students may be able to predict how large a container they would need to hold one million pennies.

2. Initiate a penny collection in your school. First decide how the pennies will be used once the collection is complete. Individual students or entire classes might suggest worthy causes, such as playground equipment, library books, or computer hardware. Some schools have donated money to local or international charities, particularly child-centered organizations such as UNICEF.

3. Invite the community to become involved: parents, organizations, other schools. As class collections grow, each class can chart or graph their progress.

4. Ask students to work with pennies or to calculate equivalent values. For example:

   ★ How many pennies make one dollar?

   ★ How many pennies make one hundred dollars? One thousand dollars?

   ★ If you have one million pennies, how many dollars do you have?

5. Encourage students to make predictions based on their data. For example, at their rate of collection, how long will it take to reach one million pennies? On approximately what date will they reach their goal of one million pennies?

6. If you wish, copy and distribute Data Sheet 8 on page 70. Ask students to mark the thermometer graph each day and record in the table the cumulative number of pennies the class has collected. If students construct their own thermometer graph, the height should be divided so that the scale is accurate, with marks representing equal amounts.

Taking It Further

How much would one million pennies weigh? Ask students how they could find out, without actually having to put a million pennies on a scale.

The Math Classroom in Action

Making It Pay

When Laurie Addeo's fourth grade class at South Country School in Bay Shore, New York, heard that an aquarium was to be built in their town, the students set to work mobilizing the community to collect a million pennies. Collection containers were placed throughout the town, and as the money came in, students graphed their progress. Working with the art teacher, they designed and printed T-shirts. They also constructed a huge model whale, which rode grandly on a float in the town's Memorial Day parade.

By the end of the year, they had 1,300,000 pennies. As a grand finale, the entire school held a Penny Celebration, for which classes created floats and banners. The choir sang "Pennies from Heaven," and local dignitaries spoke. An armored car delivered the rolled pennies to a bank. Soon afterwards, representatives of South Country School presented a check for $10,000 to the aquarium-in-progress.

Mary Costner, math specialist at Washington Avenue School in Chatham, New Jersey, wanted to coordinate a penny collection that would culminate on the day that David Schwartz was scheduled to speak at the school. With only about a month to complete the collection, she realized that the goal might be difficult to achieve, so the goal became 100,000 pennies. Classes were to collect batches of 1,000 pennies. As they did so, they posted the number of 1,000s on a large chart in the hallway.

Since she wanted a million theme, Ms. Costner added an unusual twist to her project. Once the pennies were accumulated and rolled into wrappers, students went outside and laid the rolls end-to-end in a circuitous path around the school. At recess on the day of Schwartz's visit, virtually everyone in the school—students, teachers, office staff, and the visiting author—walked the "penny route" ten times. In this way, they all had the experience of "walking a million pennies." Through a little mathematics, and exercise, the students achieved their million!

COLLECTING INVESTIGATION 3

A Motley Hundred Thousand

BIG IDEA: What kinds of things can we collect to make an assorted collection of many things? Which of these things go together?

PROCESS SKILLS: counting, collecting, sorting and classifying, recording, explaining procedures, connecting to real life

What to Do

1. Invite students to begin a collection of 10,000 or 100,000 items. This could be a grade-wide or school-wide project, depending on the size of your school. Ask students to calculate how many things each student must bring, based on the number of students that will be involved and the total number you wish to reach. Then invite each student to choose his or her own item to bring. Discuss such considerations as size, cost, and portability.

2. Make a classroom display of the items students collect. Use the items to discuss sorting and classifying: what things in the collection could go together, and in what ways? Encourage students to suggest as many different classification schemes as possible.

3. If you wish, distribute a copy of Data Sheet 9 on page 71 to each student. Ask students to make three "collections" by writing their categories and then listing things from the collection that would belong in each category. They can then use the Venn diagram, or create a giant classroom Venn diagram, to explore unique and overlapping traits.

3. When the entire grade level or school collection is displayed, ask students to see if there are any additional items they can add to the categories that were established in your class. Then invite students to determine how many such collections would be needed to have a million objects. For example, if one category had 25 items, 40,000 such groups of objects would be needed to gather one million.

Taking It Further

Begin a discussion about things that come in standard numbers, such as pairs (socks, mittens and gloves, some hair clips, pillow cases, etc.); sets of four (some foods such as pudding packs); sets of six (soft drinks, juice); and sets of twelve (eggs). Distinguish between things that come in standard numbers because of human decisions, such as those above, and things that come in standard numbers naturally—three leaflets of clover, four toes on a bird, eight legs on a spider, ten tentacles on a squid, and so on. You might post a large chart with headings for each number, and students could add items to the list over the course of several weeks.

The Math Classroom in Action

A Motley Hundred Thousand

The children of Silver Lake Elementary in Federal Way, Washington, put together a collection of 100,000 assorted items. Each child was asked to bring an equal number of items. The older students decided to calculate: they discovered that each child in the school was responsible for 173 items. The students all could decide for themselves what to bring, but all 100,000 objects would have to fit on a single large table in the gym.

Before the day appointed for showing the display, classroom discussions focused on the children's plans, leading to calculations and estimations of size and practicality of items the children might bring in.

When the display was completed, the diversity of items, in multiples of 173, was a delight for all to observe. Drops of water, baseball cards, pieces of macaroni, punched holes from colored paper, candy, pennies, popcorn, beans, seeds, a drawing of a dog with 173 lines to represent its fur, straws, cursive letters on lined paper, chocolate chips, and pine needles were but a few of the items students brought in. During the day, the entire school filed past the table to admire the display.

If Silver Lake students had made a Venn diagram for their collection, they might have used these categories: *Edible Things*, *Hard Things*, *Things Found in Nature*.

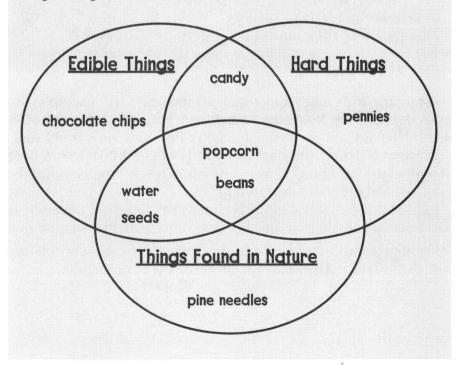

COLLECTING INVESTIGATION 4

Pop-tab-u-lation!

BIG IDEA: How can we collect one million pop tabs? How can we keep track of and store our collection?

PROCESS SKILLS: counting, collecting, recording, using place value

What to Do

1. Pop tabs, the little aluminum rings from soft drink cans, make a wonderful collectable and are useful as counters in any classroom. Ask students if they think they could collect one million pop tabs. How long would it take? How many ounces of soda or juice would each student have to drink if they used only their own cans? How would they store one million pop tabs?

2. Invite your own class and others, perhaps the entire school, to join in a pop-tab collection. As the collection grows, challenge students to devise ways to count and keep track of the number they've collected. For example, students might string sets of 100 tabs or bag by 10s, 100s, or 1,000s.

3. Using the pop tabs as counters, make piles of tens, hundreds, and thousands. Ask students to find equivalent values for larger numbers by restating them. For example:

   ten 10s is equal to _____
   ten 100s is equal to _____
   one hundred 10s is equal to _____
   one hundred 100s is equal to _____
   ten 1,000s is equal to _____
   one hundred 1,000s is equal to _____
   one thousand 10s is equal to _____

Taking It Further

★ Do some measuring and estimating with soda cans. For example, how many ounces does one can hold? How many ounces (pints, gallons) would 100 cans hold? How many ounces would 100,000 cans hold? How could students find out?

   How long is one can? How many cans would it take to run the length of the hall your classroom is on? How many would it take to go around the entire school? How could students find out?

   All the measuring tasks can be done with customary or metric units. By using both systems, students will discover how much easier it is to use metric units.

★ Investigate volume with your cans. Ask students to estimate how many cans it would take to fill a classroom, a hallway, or the entire school.

The Math Classroom in Action

Pop-tab-u-lation!

In the fall of 1992, Sybil Sevic introduced *How Much Is a Million?* to her students at Ravenel Elementary School in Seneca, South Carolina. She challenged them to bring one million pop tabs to school.

Children initially responded with boasts: "I'll bring that many in on Monday!" "We have a million cans in our garage!" "It won't take long—we drink that many cans of pop in a couple of weeks."

As classes collected pop tabs, the tabs were used for hands-on activities. Older students gathered younger children and led activities, such as skip counting, "subtracting" by counting on to find how many more would make a pile of 100, estimating what several piles put together would look like, and so forth.

As the collection progressed, children reformulated their concept of one million. When they realized it was unlikely that they would achieve their goal within the school year, they enlisted other schools in the district. Parents helped collect tabs at their places of employment. On a Saturday morning near the end of the school year, students and parents held a Pop Tab Fair. At the Fair, students participated in many mathematical activities related to counting pop tabs.

But when the total was announced, only 225,000 tabs had been collected. As the next school year began, students launched their collection efforts anew. Ravenel students went to other schools to solicit additional contributions, designed and built collection boxes for offices and stores, wrote articles for the school newspaper, and contacted the local newspaper to publicize their project.

At the second Pop Tab Fair, the collectors again found they were short of their goal. The final tally was 790,000, but the decision to continue the project was unanimous.

On November 6, 1993, students, teachers and parents gathered for their third Pop Tab Fair. To everyone's delight, the tabulation was a seven-digit number: 1,075,632!

COLLECTING INVESTIGATION 5

Pile Up the Books

BIG IDEA: How many books would one million pages fill? One million words? One million letters?

PROCESS SKILLS: counting, collecting, finding averages, calculating, recording, explaining methods

What to Do

1. Can students estimate how many pages are in a typical book in your classroom? Have students work in small groups, each group with a different book. How many of their books would it take to get one million pages? Encourage students to pick different kinds of books. Have groups report their findings.

2. Next, invite the groups to explore how many words are in a typical book in your classroom. How many books would it take to reach one million words? Again, ask students to suggest ways they could estimate, then try it, and then report to the class. Discuss possible reasons for the variety of answers, based on the type of book students used.

3. With the information of how many words there are in a typical book, suggest that the groups explore "collecting" one million letters. Ask students to estimate how many letters are on one page, and then to check by counting. They can use several pages of their book and calculate an average number. Once they have an average number of letters per page, ask them to suggest ways to find out how many pages they'd need in order to have one million letters. Why might some books have more letters per page than others?

4. For all of the above bookworm activities, encourage groups to record and report their findings, using Data Sheet 10 on page 72.

Taking It Further

Introduce concepts of averages by working with the class to determine the "average" number of pages, words, or letters in the books your groups have chosen. Find the *mean* by adding all the numbers and dividing. Find the *range* by looking at the books with the most and least pages, words, or letters. Find the *mode* by listing all numbers, in numerical order, and noting the most frequently occurring number. Find the *median* by listing all numbers, in numerical order, and noting the number in the middle of the list.

The Math Classroom in Action

Pile Up the Books

A few weeks before Christmas in 1994, students in Deb Marciano Boehm's class at Oak Lawn Elementary School in Cranston, Rhode Island, were having a classroom discussion about how lucky they were to own books. The class decided to initiate a campaign of collecting "gently used" books to donate to a local home for foster children. When other classes heard about the collection, they decided to contribute.

As the boxes of books piled up at the back of the classroom, the students wondered how many there were. Someone suggested a million. When students discovered that they had 438, and that they'd need 999,562 more books to make one million, they were dismayed. Then someone suggested they might have a million pages.

Since most of the books were primary picture books, the class decided to call all of them 32 pages long. With calculation, students saw they still weren't even close to one million pages. After reading *How Much Is A Million?*, another suggestion emerged. Perhaps there were one million words! Since no one wanted to count every word, the class determined the average number of words on a page and multiplied to find the number of words per book. When they summed the totals for each book, they were elated to find they had passed the one million mark.

Students at Yokota East Elementary School at Yokota Air Base in Japan had a twist on the idea of finding one million words: "What if we actually wrote a million words?" Participants entered their writings in a collection box, and some students took on the job of tallying up the words. Students' writings were also proudly displayed.

Creating One Million

Instead of finding one million objects, some classes have undertaken to create their own million. Students love the challenge, and this task can help them experience this large number in several dimensions. For instance, in *How Much Is a Million?*, David Schwartz offers a visual representation of the height of one million children standing on one another's shoulders and the volume of a bowl large enough to hold one million goldfish. Invite students to create their own visual representations of one million and explore the concepts of measurement, area and volume, and geometric proportions.

CREATING INVESTIGATION 1

A Million Mosaic

BIG IDEA: How can we make a mosaic of one million 1-cm squares? What shapes can we create?

PROCESS SKILLS: counting, recording, using geometric shapes

What to Do

1. Show students a 1-cm square, and ask them if they think a million of the squares would be enough, just about right, or too many to cover your classroom chalkboard. Let students make predictions, encouraging them to suggest ways they could test and confirm them.

2. Copy and distribute Data Sheet 11 on page 73 and have students use the block of 300 1-cm squares to make closer approximations of how large an area one million 1-cm squares would cover. Discuss how to find out how many squares there are if each student in the class has one sheet of squares; then let students figure it out.

3. Have students cut out the block of 300 squares. Then invite them to color the squares in a colorful pattern of their own devising. Post the rectangles edge to edge so students can see how large an area is covered.

4. Invite students to figure out possible dimensions of a one-million-square array. During the next several weeks, let students color and post additional sheets of squares; or invite other classes in the school to participate in the project. You may want to move the project to a hallway or the cafeteria or gym wall. The goal—to create a mosaic of one million squares.

Taking It Further

Show students some examples of interlocking shapes used to make a picture. These examples could include quilts, tile mosaics, and tessellations by M.C. Escher.

The Math Classroom in Action

A Million Mosaic

Math coordinator Maureen Stryker of Southern Boulevard School in Chatham, New Jersey, worked with all classes in the school to create a striking mosaic mural made of one million 1-cm squares. The 500 students of the school were each given a large sheet of paper (40-cm squares by 50-cm squares) and asked to color a pattern. The colored sheets were then arranged in a huge array, covering an entire gym wall.

Ms. Stryker used the mural as a vehicle for presenting many types of math problems. The youngest students talked about the shapes they had created in their own colorings. Older students calculated the number of squares on each sheet, the number of squares used by each class, the area of the gym wall the mural covered, the ways changing the dimensions of the mural affected area and perimeter, and so on.

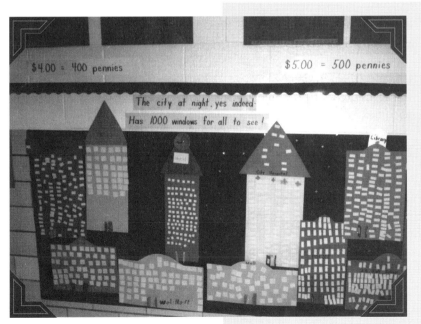

Another wall mural emerged as one of many "millions" projects at Farmington Elementary School in Culpepper, Virginia. The display of 1,000 lighted windows in a city of buildings could inspire an even larger city as a whole-school project. Or it might lead to calculations of how many more buildings would be needed for a city of one million lighted windows. Sometimes just starting the journey toward one million is enough for students to grasp how 1,000,000 relates mathematically to other numbers.

CREATING INVESTIGATION 2

The Million-Block Cube

BIG IDEA: How can we put cubes together to create a million-cube?

PROCESS SKILLS: counting, recording, calculating, constructing, justifying answers

What to Do

1. Use base-ten blocks to help students conceptualize a million-block cube. Begin with one 1-cm cube. Then show a hundred-flat. Ask students if they can tell you how many flats you would need to make a cube. Put flats together by adding one at a time so students see the construction of a thousand-cube. Ask students to tell you how many 1-cm cubes it takes to make the larger cube. How do they know?

2. Now ask students to imagine a cube with 25, then 36, squares to a side. See if they can devise a rule or formula for finding the volume—the amount of space taken up by each cube.

3. Copy and distribute Data Sheet 12 on page 74. Have students cut around the outside edges, then fold and paste or tape the tabs to create a cube. Ask: What are the dimensions of the cube? What is the volume?

4. Divide the class into groups of 4. Ask each group to figure out the volume if all of them put their cubes together. Would the volume change depending on the shape? Ask students to try various shapes and discuss their findings.

5. What if the entire class put their cubes together? Ask students to figure out the volume of a large cube made of many of their smaller cubes. Put cubes together to see what the large cube looks like. Then ask students what the dimensions would be of a cube one million centimeters square. What would it look like? Would there be room for it in the classroom? Invite students to make such a cube using their paper cubes or other materials of their choosing.

Taking It Further

You may want to talk with students more formally about volume and designations for volume. For example, the first cube they make using the reproducible contains 125 1-cm cubes; its volume is 125 cubic centimeters. Students may have already discovered the formula for finding the volume of an object: $V = l \times w \times h$.

The Math Classroom in Action

The Million-Block Cube

At the David Lubin School in Sacramento, California, Judy Carlisle's fifth grade class was working with base-ten blocks. One of the students noticed that the hundred-square (a 10-by-10 cm block) fit almost perfectly into the base of a cardboard half-gallon milk container. If two containers were cut off at a height of 10 centimeters, they could be pressed one into another, bases to the outside, to make a sturdy cube with a volume of 1,000 cubic cm. The discussion and experimentation didn't stop there. "What if we put 10 of these milk-container cubes in a row and then made 10 rows," someone suggested. "We would have a 100,000-flat."

Another student built on that idea. "And then we could stack ten of those on top of each other for a one million cube!" Soon the class had completed their plans to construct a one-meter cube of milk-container cubes, representing a volume of one million cubic centimeters.

Both teacher and students posed these and other problems related to their cubes:

★ If we have a volume of 365,000 cubes, how many more will we need to reach 1,000,000?

★ At the rate we've been bringing in milk cartons, how long will it take to collect enough to make the million-cube?

★ If we took the little 1-cm cubes apart and stacked them on top of one another, would they be as tall as the Sears Tower plus the Empire State Building plus the Eiffel Tower?

Within a few months a giant one-meter cube stood proudly at the back of the classroom. Each student was asked to make a poster that presented and solved an original problem related to the cube. Over the course of the school year, the million-cube became a kind of standard against which many things were measured and compared, from trees to mountains to clotheslines.

Fifth graders at Sullivans Elementary School in Yokosuka Naval Base in Japan made a million-cube using graph paper on a centimeter grid pattern. Both creation and construction were a challenge, but everyone in the school got a look at a cube—proudly displayed by its creators—of one million square centimeters!

33

CREATING INVESTIGATION 3

Pictures Worth a Million

BIG IDEA: What kinds of art can we create with lots of dots?

PROCESS SKILLS: counting, creating

What to Do

1. Display some pictures of paintings done with the technique known as pointillism. For example, you could show paintings by Georges Seurat, Paul Signac, or Camille Pissarro. Ask students to guess how many dots are in one of the paintings, and to speculate as to how long it might have taken the artist to create such a picture.

2. Distribute art materials: watercolor paint or tempera paint, paper, and cotton swabs. Invite students to make their own pointillist paintings.

3. Ask students to guess how many dots they used in their own paintings. Then talk with them about ways they could find out. Suggestions may range from counting every dot to making an estimate based on the number of dots in a sample area.

Taking It Further

Suggest that students gather pictures from magazines and newspapers. With the eye—or even better, with a magnifying glass—they'll see pictures composed of dots. Computer-generated images printed at home or at school will yield a similar effect. Looking at color pictures, students will even see how colors are composed of four basic colors: cyan (blue), magenta (red), yellow, and black. Ask students to choose a picture and guess how many dots might make it up. Challenge them to find a way to section off a portion of the picture to use as an average and then to figure out the total number of dots. Are there one million?

The Math Classroom in Action

Pictures Worth a Million

At University Park Elementary School in Dallas, Texas, Jan Lauer's class was studying pointillism. Jan wanted to join in the "million mania" that had swept the school, so she had the students experiment with the technique by making their own pointillist paintings. Students then made guesses as to the number of dots they had used in their own paintings.

Jan showed Georges Seurat's *Sunday Afternoon on the Island of La Grande Jatte* and students talked about how many dots they thought it had (more than a million!) and how long it took the artist to create the masterpiece.

The discussion led to further estimates of dots on a computer screen and a TV screen.

East Ward Elementary School in Downington, Pennsylvania, did a similar project with pointillist art. Students discussed how they could estimate the numbers of dots in their own art, how long it would take to put one million dots on a page, and other dotty problems.

At Farmington Elementary School in Culpepper, Virginia, students created another kind of dot picture. Here the number of dots related to a smaller number—one hundred. Younger students can count and create with 100; older students might calculate the number of pictures needed to have 1,000 or 10,000 or 100,000 or 1,000,000 dots.

Calculating One Million

There are a million ways to calculate one million! Students have looked around their classroom and school and used whatever they could find. Sometimes their work involves ordinary things, such as ceiling tiles and windows; at other times it incorporates types of food, such as candy bars or kernels of corn, or personal interests, such as basketball or television. Whatever the topic, students are eager to gather data about things in their own life. In these projects, students learn to keep careful records of their information and explore a variety of time and measurement concepts.

CALCULATING INVESTIGATION 1

In a Heartbeat

BIG IDEA: What do humans do a million or more times in a year?

PROCESS SKILLS: predicting, verifying, calculating, recording

What to Do

1. Challenge your students to think of things that humans do at least one million times per year. Give them some starting ideas if you like. For example: Does a human heart beat one million times in a year? Do humans live one million seconds? One million minutes? Do they blink one million times? Do they take one million breaths? Compile a list of as many possibilities as students can suggest.

2. Choose from the class list several ideas that are reasonable for students to actually investigate. Since no one will want to count for a year's duration, talk with the class about how they can use a smaller investigation and then calculate to get a close approximation of things humans do at least one million times in a year.

3. Divide the class into small groups and invite each group to choose a different topic to investigate. If you wish, copy and distribute Data Sheet 13 on page 75.

4. When all groups have completed their investigations, ask a volunteer from each group to report the group's methods and findings to the class. If more than one group has investigated the same thing, are the results consistent? What might account for any variations?

Taking It Further

Other ideas students might explore: Do humans swallow (or sneeze) one million times in a lifetime? These questions will lead to further calculations, plus a discussion of the number of years to assume for a "lifetime."

The Math Classroom in Action

In a Heartbeat

After hearing that it would take 23 days to count to one million, some third graders wanted to find out how long it would take them to bounce a basketball one million times.

To start the investigation, they decided to find out how long it would take to bounce the ball 100 times. They bounced furiously, and it took them only 50 seconds. They then calculated the rest:

1,000,000 ÷ 100 bounces = 10,000 sets of 100 bounces

50 seconds × 10,000 = 500,000 seconds needed to bounce 1,000,000 times

Once they had determined how many seconds were needed, they wanted to convert that large number of seconds to more useful units. They asked how many seconds were in a day:

60 seconds × 60 minutes in an hour = 3,600 seconds in one hour

3,600 seconds × 24 hours in one day = 86,400 seconds in one day

Now a simple division problem will tell them how many days it would take to achieve their goal:

500,000 seconds ÷ 86,400 seconds in one day = 5.8 days

In less than one week, they could reach one million—if they did nothing but bounce a basketball!

CALCULATING INVESTIGATION 2

Look Up! Look Down! Look All Around!

BIG IDEA: What do we have a million of in our school?

PROCESS SKILLS: predicting, verifying, calculating, recording

What to Do

1. You might explore one million by asking students what they think they have one million of in the classroom or in school. Invite speculation, and ask a volunteer to make a list on the chalkboard to record all the suggestions. Some that might arise that can be verified: holes in acoustic ceiling tiles, panes in windows, bricks or cement blocks in the walls, tiles on the floor, pencils, books, loops in the carpet. Prompt your class with some suggestions of your own that reflect the math they are studying.

2. Divide the class into small groups and ask each group to choose one suggestion from the list to investigate. Discuss the practicality of actually counting to verify any of the suggestions, and help students see how the investigation can be done by checking a small sample and then using the number to calculate an answer.

3. If the class is studying a particular topic, such as length, area, or volume, you might rephrase the question to involve these measurements and ask all groups to conduct the same investigation and then compare results. For example, students might investigate whether there are a million square inches in the floor of the gym, or if there are a million cubic centimeters in your classroom.

Taking It Further

Some students might suggest items that the class would not be able to verify on its own, such as hairs, molecules, or particles of dust. Discuss strategies for researching these subjects to get the information that would enable students to make estimates of this nature, such as the number of molecules in a given amount of matter.

The Math Classroom in Action

Look Up! Look Down! Look All Around!

In one fourth grade class, Katie decided to determine the number of holes in all the ceiling tiles in her classroom. At first she wanted to count the holes in every tile. When she started, and realized what a monumental task that would be, she decided instead to count the number of holes in half a tile and then use calculation to find the answer. She figured the total this way:

> There are a million blades of grass, germs, people, pennies, bugs, rocks, but there aren't a million dots on our ceiling — Oh, no....
>
> 23 by 23
> 529
> 4.22 Approx
> Multi dot 224
> 16
> 23
> Rows 368
>
> 192 tiles   26 tiles   384 tiles   32 tiles
>
> 101,568 + 15,972 + 86,016 + 11,776 = 219,588

306 holes in half a tile × 2 = 612 holes in a tile

612 holes × 93 tiles in the classroom = 56,916 holes

Since she hadn't reached one million, Katie decided to add all six fourth grade classrooms. She did this, and found there were 341,496 holes all together. Seeing she was about one-third of the way to one million, Katie added on the six classrooms each of grades one and two, and finally reached her goal:

341,496 × 3 = 1,024,488

So, 18 classrooms represented one million holes—and a few more!

We brainstormed things in our school we think we have one million of... Then we investigated to discover how much of each there really is... Then we graphed our results. Each square represents 1,000, and the whole graph represents 1,000,000.

Another fourth grade class wanted to find out if their school contained one million floor tiles. They worked in pairs as they scattered throughout the school, counting tiles in classrooms, hallways, offices, and the cafeteria. When all the tiles were counted and added, however, the total was just 53,000 tiles. Students were amazed to find, with the help of a calculator, that they would need another 18 schools their size, or another 18 floors on their own school, to top one million floor tiles.

CALCULATING INVESTIGATION 3

A School for Millions

BIG IDEA: How many schools would we need for one million kids?

PROCESS SKILLS: predicting, verifying, calculating, recording

What to Do

1. Invite your class to guess how many students are enrolled in your school. Then determine some ways to verify this, from surveying every class to using an average number per grade and calculating.

2. With the number of students in your own school to represent an average, challenge your students to find out how many schools would be needed for one million students. Students can record statistics for your own class and school, and then use repeated subtraction or division to find the number of such schools that would be needed to house one million students.

Taking It Further

★ Once students have determined how many schools it would take for a million kids, they can do some research to determine if there are that many schools in their district, city, county, or state.

★ Have students conduct other school-based investigations regarding space for things—other than students! They might calculate the number of books in the library and see how that number stacks up against space for one million books. They can also find out the number of tables that fit in the cafeteria, of seats in the school auditorium, of people that fit on the bleachers in the gym, of desks in the classroom, and so on. Armed with data, they can relate each place to the space needed for one million.

978,625 978,626 978,627 978,628 978,629 978,630 978,631 978,632 978,333 978,634

BIG Number Fact

A school in the Philippines has 19,738 students enrolled. How many schools of this size would it take to enroll one million students?

The Math Classroom in Action

A School for Millions

Some fourth graders decided to see how many schools it would take to represent one million kids. They decided to use their own school of 1,100 students as the standard size. At first they began counting sets of twenty:

Number of Schools	Number of Students
1	1,100
20	22,000
40	44,000
60	66,000
80	88,000
100	110,000

When they got this far, they discussed the relationship between 100,000 and 1,000,000. Since 10 x 100,000 = 1,000,000, they multiplied 110,000 by 10 to arrive at 1,100,000 students for 1,000 schools.

Some students wanted a more accurate picture. They revised the original estimate by subtracting successive groups of students and schools:

Number of Schools	Number of Students
1,000	1,100,000
−20	−22,000
980	1,078,000
−20	−22,000
960	1,056,000
−20	−22,000
940	1,034,000
−20	−22,000
920	1,012,000

Or, 920 schools would be needed for about one million kids.

Ravenel Elementary School students Sean and Drew did an investigation into school size. Sean reported, "The biggest problem we had was finding out how many students were in Ravenel. I was looking up the students in the Postal Directory when my teacher suggested that I just go to the office and ask the computer lady how many students were enrolled in school. That was the first thing we did. Then we divided one million by that number and got 2,141. Then we made a picture graph. Another problem we had was making all the little men to represent the school. We didn't want to make that many men so we used each man to be 100 schools. I enjoyed working with big numbers."

CALCULATING INVESTIGATION 4

It Seems Like a Million Days!

BIG IDEA: Do we go to school for one million days?

PROCESS SKILLS: predicting, verifying, measuring, calculating, recording

What to Do

1. Ask your students to guess how many days they go to school each year. Tell them the policy for your district if they don't know. Most school districts have students attend for around 180 days.

2. With that information, ask them to predict whether any students go to school for one million days. What about students who go to college? Graduate school? After they've made some guesses, invite them to calculate to find out. They can take the number of years they spend in elementary school, middle school, high school, college, and even graduate school, and find the number of days.

3. Once they have a number of days for school attendance, students can use a calculator to determine how many years they would have to go to school to attend one million days. You can use Data Sheet 14 on page 76 for students to record their work.

This is also an excellent opportunity to do some mental math, using 200 days rather than 180. Students can figure out mentally that in ten years (ten grades) a student would go to school for a bit less than 2,000 days. So even if they went to school for 20 years, including college and graduate school, they would be under 4,000 days—far less than a million, even if it seems like more!

Taking It Further

Students might investigate how much time is spent on school-related activities, or even how much time it takes them to walk to school, and then relate these numbers to one million. Another question might involve the number of steps taken on the way to school (or in the school building) each day or week or year. Do we walk a million steps to get to school in a year? In our entire time in school, from kindergarten to 12th grade? How long does it take to walk a million steps?

The Math Classroom in Action

It Seems Like a Million Days!

Some fifth graders tackled the problem of the number of days in school by calculating each segment of their education.

elementary school = 180 × 6 = 1,080 days
middle school = 180 × 3 = 540 days
high school = 180 × 4 = 720 days
college = 180 × 4 = 720 days

With this typical education program, students discovered that for 17 years of schooling they had only reached 3,060 days.

Determined to reach one million, some students suggested adding on preschool and daycare. Others pointed out that to become a doctor a person might spend 10 years in college. Still they were nowhere near one million days.

Using a calculator, students divided 1,000,000 by 180 and discovered that they would have to go to school for 5,556 years to reach one million days. At the conclusion of the investigation, one student remarked, "A million is more than meets the eye!"

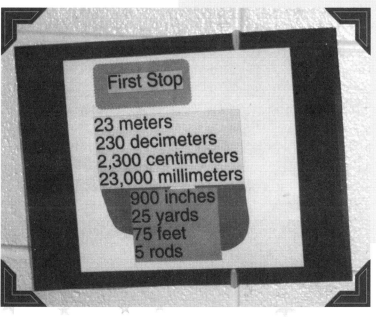

First Stop

23 meters
230 decimeters
2,300 centimeters
23,000 millimeters
900 inches
25 yards
75 feet
5 rods

One way to get an understanding of one million is physically. Students at Frontier Elementary School in Colorado Springs, Colorado, decided to "walk a million"—in this case, a million millimeters. Students figured out the distance that one million millimeters covered and then marched the route, stopping at predetermined spots. This activity reinforced measurement concepts and understanding of metric units.

CALCULATING INVESTIGATION 5

Water, Water Everywhere— And Too Many Drops to Drink

BIG IDEA: What do we eat or drink a million of in a lifetime?
PROCESS SKILLS: predicting, verifying, calculating, recording

What to Do

1. Invite students to guess what things it might be reasonable to assume humans consume in a lifetime. Open the discussion with a few examples, if necessary: for example, do we drink one million gallons of water? Do we consume one million calories? Do we eat one million slices of bread? Encourage students to make wide-ranging suggestions. Record their responses on the chalkboard, and after each one ask the class to discuss whether the suggestion seems reasonable.

2. With the class, identify which suggestions would be possible to verify. Assign students to small groups, and have each group choose one of the ideas to investigate. Encourage them to work together to determine what to use as baseline numbers in their calculations. They may need to do this by taking an average for their group. For example, they should use the average number of glasses of water drunk in a day, or the average number of slices of bread eaten in a day.

3. If you want, use Data Sheet 13 on page 75 for students to record their work and their findings. Allow each group to explain their task, their assumptions, and their findings to the class.

Taking It Further

Students could investigate water in a number of other interesting ways. Give these facts, and have students find questions and answers related to one million.

★ A running faucet can use up to 5 gallons per minute. At that rate, how long would it take to use one million gallons?

★ Washing dishes with the tap running can use up to 30 gallons of water. How many gallons would be used in one year? Ask students to investigate how much water is used if basins are used for washing and rinsing. How much water would be saved in one year?

★ A standard shower head uses 5 to 7 gallons of water per minute. How many gallons of water does an average family use each day? How long would it take to use one million gallons of water? If the family installed a low-flow shower head that uses 2.5 gallons of water per minute, how would that affect their consumption of water for showers?

The Math Classroom in Action

Water, Water Everywhere— And Too Many Drops to Drink

Some fourth grade students enthusiastically tackled the Water, Water project. One student wondered if a person could drink a million gallons of water in a lifetime. To figure this out, the class decided they needed to know how much the average person drinks in one day. At first their estimates ranged from one to ten gallons, but they finally agreed to use one half gallon per day as reasonable.

Students quickly determined that if it took them two days to drink one gallon of water, it would take two million days to drink the one million gallons of water. They then figured out how many days are in the life of a person who lives to age 85. Calculating 85 x 365 = 31,025 days, they realized that even if they lived to age 85 they could not drink a million gallons of water.

One Million Drops

The way I learned that ten gallons of water equals 1 million drops is this.
First I counted how many drops of water can fit into a teaspoon. Then I counted how many teaspoons of water fit into 1 cup. I multiplyed the number of drops in a teaspoon by the number of teaspoons in a cup. I know that there are 16 cups in a gallon so I multiplyed the number of drops in a cup by 16. This number was 996,766 which rounded to 100,000. I multiplyed that by 10 and got 1,000,000. So 10 gallons is a little more than 1,000,000 drops.

At Indian Lane Elementary School in Media, Pennsylvania, even the school dietitian got involved in one of the school's millions projects. Working with a class, she and students calculated the caloric content of food shipped into the school's food service, and made an impressive display of empty boxes that had contained one million calories. This activity led to additional projects involving food and nutrition.

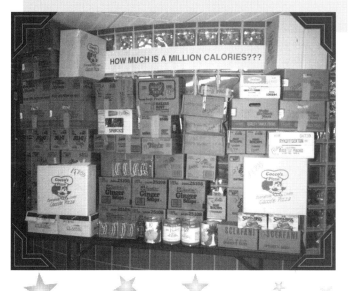

HOW MUCH IS A MILLION CALORIES???

Students at Eagle Valley Elementary School in Eagle, Colorado, did a series of calculations in order to explore a million of various items. Among other investigations, student sleuths investigated the following: pieces of cereal per box to calculate the number of boxes that would hold one million pieces; entry words per page in a dictionary to calculate the number of words in a dictionary, and the number of dictionaries for one million entry words; drops of water in a cup to calculate the number of cups that would hold one million drops.

45

CALCULATING INVESTIGATION 6

And Now a Word from Our Sponsor

BIG IDEA: How many days (weeks, years) would it take to watch one million hours of television?

PROCESS SKILLS: predicting, verifying, calculating, recording

What to Do

1. Interesting big number investigations can revolve around the amount of time students spend watching TV. Ask your students to list how much time, in numbers of minutes, they spend each day watching TV. (Ask students to report total time, not consecutive amounts of time.) You might ask someone to tally or graph the responses by number of hours, so the class can see at a glance how many students watch for one half, one, two, three (or on to the maximum number of hours) hours a day.

2. Use an average figure to represent the number of hours per day for the class, or ask each student to use his or her own response, to calculate how long it would take them (first in days, then in numbers of weeks, months, and years) to watch one million hours of television. Students can record their findings on Data Sheet 15 on page 77.

3. In addition to the time spent watching TV, students are usually interested in finding out how much of that time is spent watching commercials. By observing and recording the number of minutes in a 30-minute program devoted to commercials, students can calculate how much of their total TV time is consumed by commercials.

Taking It Further

Other kinds of TV data students might like to investigate:

★ How many hours of television watching does the average person accumulate by the time they are 18 years old? At that rate, how many hours does the average person watch TV in a lifetime?

★ How long would it take to watch one million commercials?

978,625 978,626 978,627 978,628 978,629 978,630 978,631 978,632 978,333 978,634

BIG Number Fact

From age 3 to age 18, children in the United States see about 350,000 TV commercials. Students might like to figure out how many commercials are seen per year, and how many years it would take to see one million.

978,640 978,641 978,642 978,643 978,644 978,645 978,646 978,647 978,648 978,649

The Math Classroom in Action

And Now a Word from Our Sponsor

A group of fourth grade students, frustrated with the number of commercials they had to watch on television, decided to calculate how long it would take them to watch one million commercials. They took a survey of how many hours kids watch TV, especially during the summer. (Their numbers represented the total number of hours per day, not consecutive amounts of time.) They decided to use some of the highest responses as the basis for their calculations: Monday to Thursday, 7 hours; Friday, 8 hours; Saturday, 10 hours; Sunday, 8 hours. A small group then watched television for one hour at home and counted 38 commercials. They used a calculator to help them solve the rest:

38 commercials × 7 hours × 4 days = 1,064 commercials
38 commercials × 8 hours × 2 days = 608 commercials
38 commercials × 10 hours × 1 day = 320 commercials
Total = 2,052 commercials in one week

1,000,000 ÷ 2,052 = 488 weeks

488 weeks ÷ 52 = 9.4 years to watch one million commercials

CALCULATING ONE MILLION

CALCULATING INVESTIGATION 7

We Love Food!

BIG IDEA: How long would it take to consume one million of our favorite food?

PROCESS SKILLS: predicting, verifying, calculating, recording

What to Do

1. It's a rare child who doesn't have a favorite kind of candy. Take a classroom poll to find out about your students' favorites. As students share their responses, make a list. Then ask one student or a small group to make a graph showing the results.

2. Using students' responses, invite them to speculate how long it would take to consume one million of their favorites. Encourage them to establish some reasonable benchmarks to use for calculations: for example, if the favorite is a bar candy, how many bars would they reasonably consume in a day? If it is a bag of candy, such as M&Ms, how many bags would they reasonably consume in a day?

3. As part of their investigations, any students who are using bags of candy can also find out how many pieces they get in a bag and then calculate the actual time per piece for that number of pieces.

4. Ask students to share their findings and to explain how they determined their results.

Taking It Further

Some other food facts students might investigate:

★ Is it possible to eat one million pieces of a certain food in your lifetime (such as pieces of a certain kind of cereal)? How about one million ice cream cones?

★ If you laid one million bananas (or other food) end-to-end, how many miles would they stretch?

★ How long would it take a typical pizza parlor to sell one million pizzas?

978,625 978,626 978,627 978,628 978,629 978,630 978,631 978,632 978,333 978,634

BIG Number Facts

★ Americans eat, on average, a total of about 5 tons of candy each day. A small car weighs about 2 tons, so that's equivalent to the weight of 2½ small cars!

★ Americans eat more than 400,000 bushels of bananas each day.

978,640 978,641 978,642 978,643 978,644 978,645 978,646 978,647 978,648 978,649

978,650 978,651 978,652 978,653 978,654

978,635 978,636 978,637 978,638 978,639

The Math Classroom in Action

We Love Food!

Third-grader Stephen really liked jelly beans. He decided to figure out how long it would take him to eat one million of his favorite candy. He decided he would eat two packs per day. Stephen and his partner found out there were 25 jelly beans in a pack, so he would eat 50 jelly beans a day. With some calculation, he figured it would take 54.9, or about 55 years, to eat that many jelly beans.

Matthew figured, "You know, in 55 years I'll be 63 years old!" It would take a great part of a lifetime to consume that many jelly beans. He was not even certain that he would be able to sustain that kind of eating. "After eating fifty jelly beans every day for a couple of years, " he said, "I'd probably be sick to death of them. I don't think that I could ever eat a million of them."

Alas, one million can be too much of a good thing!

CALCULATING INVESTIGATION 8

Your Name Is One in a Million!

BIG IDEA: How many times would we have to write our names to total one million letters?

PROCESS SKILLS: predicting, verifying, calculating, recording

What to Do

1. Ask each student to write her or his full name and count the total number of letters. Survey the class to determine information about the number of letters in people's names. For example, how many letters are in the longest name? the shortest name? What is the average number of letters in a name? You might graph the data to show the range of numbers of letters and the number of students having a particular number of letters in their names. Is there a number that is most common? Is that the same as the average number?

2. With their own name, have students calculate the number of times they would have to write their complete name to have written one million letters. Gather ideas from students as to how they might determine this number. Students should see that division is the most efficient way to calculate, but that repeated subtraction, a form of division, will also work.

3. After each student has finished his or her own investigation, ask volunteers to report their findings to the class.

Taking It Further

An interest in letters could lead to other investigations, such as finding out how many names/letters there are in your city's phone directory. What would be a good way to calculate this? You could also tie in a reading project, like one of those described on pages 58–60 of this book, with a calculation of how long it would take the class to read one million letters, words, or pages. Or ask students to figure out how long it would take to write their own name one million times.

978,625 978,626 978,627 978,628 978,629 978,630 978,631 978,632 978,333 978,634

BIG Number Fact

The longest name to appear on a birth certificate is:

Rhoshandiatellyneshiaunneveshenk Koyaanisquatsiuth Williams.

The name belongs to a girl, born in 1984.

978,640 978,641 978,642 978,643 978,644 978,645 978,646 978,647 978,648 978,649

The Math Classroom in Action

Your Name Is One in a Million!

The students in one fourth grade class predicted that if they counted the letters in the students' and teachers' names at school they could reach one million letters. They used the school directory, which contained the names of all the students and teachers in kindergarten through fifth grade, and gave each other certain pages to count. Once everyone had finished their own pages, the class added the totals together and found a grand total of 10,317 letters.

Since they still wanted to relate the figure to one million, they decided to find out how many pages in the directory it would take to reach one million letters. As they looked at their initial counts, they saw that each page of the directory had a different number of letters, so they decided to find the average as a number to work with. They divided 10,317 by 19 pages and found 543 to be the average number of letters per page. When they divided 1,000,000 by 543 they were astounded to find that they would need a directory of 1,842 pages to represent one million letters.

When students think about words and letters they often turn to the dictionary. In a fourth grade class the students decided to add the words in their dictionaries to see if they had one million words. They found there were approximately 40 words on a page (the entry words, not the total number of words) and calculated the rest:

40 words per page × 1,058 pages = 42,320 words in one dictionary

42,320 words × 25 dictionaries = 1,058,000 words in a class set of dictionaries

CALCULATING INVESTIGATION 9

How Far Is One Million?

BIG IDEA: How can we measure one million units to help us picture the number 1,000,000?

PROCESS SKILLS: predicting, verifying, measuring, calculating, recording

What to Do

1. It's often difficult for students to imagine one million of a given measurement unit. Display a yardstick or meter stick and ask students to speculate about distances such as one million centimeters (or inches); one million feet, yards or meters; one million kilometers or miles. If we started at school and walked that distance, where would we end up?

2. Using either metric units or customary units, ask students to come up with a way to convert one million inches (or centimeters) into units that are more useful when dealing with large distances (kilometers or miles, for example).

$$12 \text{ inches} = 1 \text{ foot}$$
$$5{,}280 \text{ feet} = 1 \text{ mile}$$
$$\text{so, } 1 \text{ mile} = 12 \times 5{,}280, \text{ or } 63{,}360 \text{ inches}$$
$$1{,}000{,}000 \div 63{,}360 = 15.78$$

So, one million inches would be 15.8 or about 16 miles.

3. Using a city or state map, locate your school site and use the map key to find some places that would be about 16 miles away. You can use a compass to inscribe a circle with a radius of 16 miles, so students can see what locations they would be able to reach if they traveled one million inches.

4. Have students use other measurement equivalents for customary and metric units of length to calculate the number of miles or kilometers for the questions given on Data Sheet 16 on page 78. You can provide the following information, or students can use their math books to look up measurement equivalents.

Customary	Metric
1 mile = 63,360 inches	1 kilometer = 100,000 centimeters
5,280 feet	10,000 decimeters
1,760 yards	1,000 meters

Once students have done some measurements and calculations, ask them which measuring system they like better, and why.

The Math Classroom in Action

How Far Is One Million?

A third grade class was interested in knowing how far a million inches would be. They decided to convert the answer to miles so they could better understand just how far the distance was. First they used the quarter-mile track behind their school. Since the track was not quite accurate, their measurements in inches and calculations gave them an answer of about 17 miles for one million inches.

Their teacher then helped them calculate, and they discovered that one million inches is 15.8 (or about 16) miles. When students speculated about what was 16 miles from the school, they mentioned familiar landmarks, such as stores and housing developments, that were only 4 to 8 miles away. With the use of a county map, students found that 16 miles was the distance to the county fairgrounds.

In a third grade class in South Carolina, students decided to use toy railroad tracks to think about one million. When their teacher asked them to predict how far they thought a million eleven-inch tracks would stretch, they ventured a variety of distances: "to the top of my cul-de-sac;" "to the fifth grade;" "all the way around the whole school;" "to Charlotte;" "to New York City." With the help of a calculator, they made the following discovery:

$$11 \text{ inches} \times 1{,}000{,}000 = 11{,}000{,}000 \text{ inches}$$
$$11{,}000{,}000 \text{ inches} \div 12 = 916{,}66.66 \text{ feet}$$
$$916{,}66.66 \text{ feet} \div 5{,}280 \text{ feet} = 173.6 \text{ miles, or about } 174 \text{ miles}$$

But how far was 174 miles? With a map of South Carolina at hand, students cut a piece of ribbon to represent 174 miles. They placed one end at the location of their school and stretched the other end to see how far it would reach. They discovered they could indeed reach Charlotte, Savannah, or the Great Smoky Mountains.

With a map of the United States, they used the new distance scale to cut a new ribbon representing 174 miles. The ribbon did not reach to New York City. But students noted that as the map covered more territory their ribbon got shorter, leading to some important generalizations about scale and proportion.

CALCULATING INVESTIGATION 10

Walk One Million

BIG IDEA: How long would it take if you walked one million steps, and how far would you get?

PROCESS SKILLS: predicting, verifying, measuring, calculating, recording

What to Do

1. Along with measurement of distances involving one million can come some interesting investigations of time involving millions. For example, invite students to estimate how long it would take to walk one million steps, or paces. Record their predictions. Then discuss how they could use calculations to figure this out without actually taking one million paces.

2. Students should realize that one way to calculate the time is to choose a uniform length (or distance) as the basis for their calculations. They might use the length of a school hallway, the perimeter of the gym floor, or the length of an indoor or outdoor running track. Have students first measure the distance they will walk, and then determine the time it takes to pace out that distance. If students suggest that not everyone will take the same amount of time, have several volunteers walk the distance at a normal rate and then determine an average time. (You might want to assign pairs of students to choose their own length, time one another, and complete the calculations.)

3. Once students know the time for one circuit of their chosen length, they can calculate the time it would take to walk one million steps. Have students record the information using Data Sheet 17 on page 79.

Taking It Further

Some other time-related investigations with school items: How long would it take to use one million pencils? Straws? How long would it take to read one million words? How long would it take to sell one million school lunches?

The Math Classroom in Action

Walk One Million

In one school, students decided to take advantage of the mile track to show the magnitude of one million. They investigated the time it would take them to walk one million steps. After walking around the mile track one time, they found that it took them a little over 2,000 steps to cover the mile in a time span of forty minutes. Calculating the rest:

1,000,000 steps ÷ 2,000 steps per mile = 500 miles

500 miles × 40 minutes per mile = 20,000 minutes

20,000 minutes ÷ 60 minutes in an hour = 333.33 hours

333.33 hours ÷ 24 hours in a day = 13.88 days walking (nonstop) to walk one million steps

Students figured that even walking 7 hours a day, it would take them 47.6 days to walk one million steps. No one was ready to volunteer!

CALCULATING INVESTIGATION 11

One Million in the News

BIG IDEA: How can we use the newspaper to investigate one million?
PROCESS SKILLS: predicting, verifying, calculating, recording

What to Do

1. Display a newspaper page, and ask students to list as many ways as they can think of that numbers are used in the news. Students may suggest sports scores, weather data, distances or population figures in news articles, and so on. Students may notice that some parts of the paper use numbers more often, and in different ways, than others. Encourage them to look in news, sports, business, living, advertising, real estate, and other sections. Ask students to predict how often numbers are used on each page of the various sections of the newspaper.

2. Now distribute a newspaper page to each student (or limit them to front pages only) and ask students to find and circle all the numbers on their page. Discuss how they could find the average number of numbers for a page of front pages. Be sure students notice and discuss what sorts of numbers are "big" (which you can define as numbers of one million or more) and which are small. Can they come up with any generalizations about what kinds of news items utilize big numbers? What does this tell them about the usefulness of big numbers?

3. With Data Sheet 18 on page 80, students can record their findings and their conclusions about the use of numbers in the news. What kinds of newspaper pages utilize numbers most often? What types of pages have the least use of numbers? Why do students think this is the case?

Taking It Further

Perhaps the most common use of numbers in the news involves money. As they examine newspaper pages, see what categories students can come up with, such as *prices* of things (from consumer goods to public works projects, school budgets, taxes, stock prices), *costs* (damage caused by disasters), *salaries* (especially those of celebrities whose salaries are often in the millions!) and others.

Students can also find advertising figures in the newspaper, then cut out and add examples of products and costs to see if they can spend one million (pennies, or dollars).

The Math Classroom in Action

One Million in the News

At Ravenel Elementary School, in Seneca, South Carolina, students worked with mathematics teacher Sybil Sevic to investigate millions in a variety of ways—including using the newspaper. Afterward, students wrote about the activity.

Elizabeth noted, "I have made a bulletin board with some other people. We all did the same thing, but with articles of the newspaper. We circled on one page all the numbers. I had a problem. It took too long to circle all the numbers and add the numbers. Then some of us had to use part of the page and estimate that the rest of the page parts had the same number. It was tiring, but fun."

Jamie reported, "It's fun to do this newspaper counting stuff. Sometimes it's hard to find some numbers when they're right in front of your face. I'm going to try it at home because it's so fun."

Reading One Million—
A Heyday for Bookworms

Because one million is a BIG number, "million mania" can lead to some BIG reading projects. What better way to link reading and math than a reading incentive program based on the number 1,000,000—in pursuit of a collective goal such as one million pages or one million minutes of reading.

Since students must quantify and record their reading totals, an abundance of data flows into the school on a daily basis. Visitors to schools that are undertaking a "million" reading incentive may be greeted by large "thermometer" graphs. In other schools, bar graphs or pictographs lining the corridors communicate the progress of each grade or class. Here is nothing less than the essence of what elementary education should be: great quantities of reading, and equal doses of mathematics used as a tool for communicating real information.

Many "million" reading programs involve parents and siblings, and some even reach out to the greater community. Most "million" reading-incentive programs have involved an entire school, but you can easily adapt them to a single class by cutting the goal from one million to a lower (but still impressive) number.

Reading Goal—40 Minutes Per Day
John Pettibone School
New Milford, Connecticut

Anyone visiting John Pettibone School in March, 1995, would have known immediately that something special was going on. Corridors were ablaze with signs, charts, graphs, and artwork—all attesting to a student body that had turned off the televisions and turned on to books. "SPEED LIMIT 40 M.P.D." shouted signs designed to resemble highway speed signs. But in this case the speed was not a maximum traveling pace but a minimum reading pace: 40 minutes per day. Each morning students were abuzz with talk—not about sit-coms they had seen but about minutes of reading they had done!

Outside classrooms, bulletin boards displayed the titles and covers of books the children had just completed. Taped to the wall outside each room, large envelopes were stuffed with "reading coupons" on which readers had recorded their daily totals. Fourth and fifth graders collected the coupons each day, tallied the amounts, and graphed the data.

John Pettibone's "March to a Million" was launched March 1st. On the 25th of March, the school principal beat a drum over the P.A. system to announce the school's achievement of its goal.

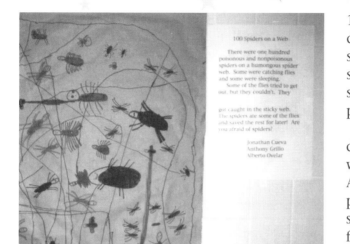

"Hall of Hundreds"

**Rolling Valley Elementary School
Springfield, Virginia**

Some schools have encouraged writing activities along with their millions theme. At Rolling Valley Elementary School, students started with a more manageable number—100—and created a "Hall of Hundreds." On display were illustrations of 100 of a given object or category, along with stories and poetry about those things. Math, reading, and writing rolled into one fun project!

Flying Higher

**Bradford Elementary School
Pueblo, Colorado**

In one of the most impressive collective reading projects we know, fourth grade teacher Elaine Madrid enlisted the school principal, her teaching colleagues, and eventually the entire community, challenging them to join the "Bradford Is Worth a Million Community Reading Challenge." As a novel way of inviting people to join the project, students held a balloon launch. Invitations were tied to helium balloons (illegal in some communities), encouraging community members to come to Bradford to read aloud to small groups of students. Principal Carmen Peralta declared that

15 minutes of every school day would be devoted to reading, and students read outside school as well. A large graph was set up, and students colored in a book-stack graph to show their progress toward reading a million pages.

Once the goal was achieved, some students wondered how high 1,000,000 pages would stack if piled on top of one another. After taking measurements and making computations, Mrs. Madrid's class estimated the stack of one million pages would reach 290 feet in the air.

To help students understand such a height, a real estate company came to the rescue with its own balloon—a hot-air balloon. On the day David Schwartz visited Bradford, the Remax balloon also arrived. Its mission: to fly 290 feet above the school grounds. The fourth grade students had measured a ribbon 290 feet long. They attached one end to the balloon's basket, and as the balloon headed skyward, the ribbon unfurled to mark the height of one million pages of reading.

Several weeks later, Mrs. Madrid's class was invited to the Colorado State House and recognized on the floor of the state Senate for their reading achievement. Bradford had truly risen to new heights!

Reading and Math Do Mix

Visitacion Valley Middle School
San Francisco, California

After hearing David Schwartz speak at a math conference, one middle school math teacher started a million-minute reading incentive at her school. Reading teachers found themselves doing mathematics in their classrooms, while math teachers found themselves stressing the importance of reading. Of course, the math teachers found ways to incorporate the reading project into their own curriculum. Students computed average minutes read per week, average cumulative minutes read by the different grades, percent of projected goals achieved, and percent of the final goal. Data were entered into computers and used to draw line graphs whose slopes were analyzed to determine reading rates. Strips of adding machine tape, one millimeter for every minute read, were mounted in the hallway. The school even set up a web site for interested parties to track their progress!

Read to Rise

E. R. Taylor School
San Francisco, California

San Francisco businessman Bruce McKinney offered this school an unusual incentive to read: $10,000 to buy books for the school library if the 350 students would read, collectively, 1,000,000 pages. The school accepted the challenge, and a giant bookworm was constructed to document the reading progress. As completion neared, McKinney

upped the stakes: $25,000 if students could read 2.5 million pages. By the end of one school year they had reached one million, and students voted to keep reading. As Mr. McKinney said, students who read will "rise in life, rise in their expectations, and rise to become college bound."

See Us Dunk Mr. See

Arroyo Seco Elementary School
Livermore, California

Here was an unusual reading incentive project—at least for school principal Mr. See. Each student was encouraged to read 1,000 pages to gain admission into the 1,000 Pages Club. For each page read, students "earned" two drops of water toward a future dunk tank. The 500 students in the school would thereby generate 1,000,000 drops of water. Students graphed their progress, and eventually they got to dunk Mr. See. Their poem tells the story:

You add water by the drop
'Till the tank is at its top.
You can add two drops for every page you read.
We will mark it on our gauge—
Keeping track at every stage
'Till we've counted up the million drops we need.
When the tank has reached its limit,
He'll be ready then to swim it.
We'll be watching as we soak our Mr. See.
But the knowledge that we gain—
Reading will expand the brain
And we'll get a googol fun—and all for free!

Create Your Own "Millionaire's Club": Great Books to Read

Aker, Suzanne. *What Comes in 2's, 3's and 4's?* **Simon and Schuster, 1990.**

This book introduces readers to things in the world that come in sets of 2, 3, and 4 by showing a delightful range of objects: two images in the mirror, two pieces of bread on a sandwich, and two ways to go on a seesaw. There are three lights on a traffic light, three primary colors, and three meals to eat each day. Students will want to make their own lists of objects that come in particular sets, and then use the ideas to do some calculations regarding millions.

Alexander, Martha. *Where Does the Sky End, Grandpa?* **Harcourt Brace Jovanovich, 1992.**

Grandpa and his young grandchild take a walk and ask many questions about the world: where is forever, how far can birds fly, does the sky ever end, does the sea go on forever? Such questions can lead to some interesting large number explorations.

Anno, Mitsumasa. *Anno's Mysterious Multiplying Jar.* **Philomel, 1983.**

Anno's marvelous jar leads to some large numbers in a hurry. Readers look into a jar that contains a sea with one island; on the island are two countries; within each country are three mountains; on each mountain are four kingdoms, and so on. It's a story about factorials and how they grow to be very large!

_____. *Anno's Magic Seeds.* **Philomel, 1995.**

A young lad named Jack encounters a wizard who gives him two golden seeds. Jack eats one, and isn't hungry for a year. He plants the other, and it produces two more seeds. This is a story of seeds that keep producing, and the mathematical consequences.

Barry, David. *The Rajah's Rice.* **W. H. Freeman, 1994.**

When Chandra, the official bather of the Rajah's elephants, saves them from a serious illness, she requests a reward more costly than the Rajah realizes. She points to a checkerboard hanging on the wall and asks that she be given one grain of rice for the first square on the board, two grains for the second square, and double that amount each day until the 64 squares on the board are used. When the Rajah eventually runs out of rice and realizes the impossibility of the request, he agrees to give the villagers back their land in exchange for being released from his promise to Chandra.

Dee, Ruby. *Two Ways to Count to Ten.* **Holt, 1988.**

In this story the lion, mighty king of the jungle, is getting tired and must pick a successor. He holds a contest, challenging the other animals to throw his javelin into the air and count to ten before it hits the ground. In turn the animals try and fail—until the clever antelope counts by 2s and wins the contest.

Firch, David. *The King's Chessboard.* **Dial, 1988.**

This book tells the same tale as *The Rajah's Rice*, but the characters are different. In this case the king wishes to reward his grand counselor for all his wise advice. The counselor requests a reward—based on the doubling principle—using the squares of the king's chessboard. The king learns to be a bit more humble when he realizes the impossibility of granting such a costly reward. (A similar story is told in Helena Pittman's *A Grain of Rice.* Bantam, 1992.)

Giganti, Paul. *Notorious Numbers.* **Scholastic, 1994.**

This is a good companion to Aker's book. With some larger numbers, it provides a numerical look at the world and invites students to find items in their own experience that are grouped in particular ways.

Hertzberg, Hendrik. *One Million.* **Random House, 1993.**

This wonderful resource is a book composed of one million dots! It also presents interesting facts that help students compare the relative size of large numbers.

Lasky, Kathryn. *The Librarian Who Measured the Earth*. **Little, Brown, 1994.**

This book provides a fascinating glimpse into the life of Eratosthenes, the famous Greek scholar who made many discoveries about Earth (and who also was the chief librarian at the great library in Alexandria, Egypt). This is the story of how Eratosthenes calculated the circumference of Earth—a measurement that was only 200 miles different from our own calculations today.

Mathews, Judith. *Two of Everything*. **Albert Whitman, 1993.**

A poor farmer digs up an ancient pot from his field, drags it home, and tosses his purse with his last five gold coins inside it for safe keeping. After a day, he discovers that the pot contains two identical purses with five coins in each of them. The farmer and his wife grow rich by continually placing coins in this magic doubling pot. They even inadvertently fall into the pot themselves but all ends happily when the two husbands and two wives become good friends and live next door to one another in identical houses.

Nesbil, E. *Melisande*. **Harcourt Brace, 1989.**

A princess cursed by an evil fairy is born beautiful but bald. When she is granted one wish, she asks for golden hair that is a yard long, which will grow an inch every day and twice as fast when it is cut. The wish leads to some problems of mathematical proportions!

Schwartz, David M. *G Is for Googol: A Math Alphabet Book*. **Tricycle Press, 1998.**

This exploration of math words leads to problem solving and mind-bending mathematical activities. Some of the entries are common math words: B is for Binary, P is for Probability. Other entries are delightful and humorous surprises: I is for If, and W is for When are we ever gonna use this stuff, anyway?

_____. *How Much Is a Million?* **Lothrop, Lee & Shepard, 1985.**

A beautifully illustrated book with speculations and wonderings about millions: the height of one million kids on one another's shoulders; the size of a bowl for one million goldfish; the time it would take to count from one to one billion; and more. The inspiration for this book!

_____. *If You Made a Million*. **Lothrop, Lee & Shepard, 1989.**

Marvelosissimo the Mathematical Magician leads readers on a jubilant journey to help them understand the mathematics of money and the connections between earning, saving, and spending—beginning with a penny and ending with a million dollars. Readers also learn about the weight of one million dollars in quarters, and the height of one million dollar bills.

Thaler, Mike. *Owly*. **Harper and Row, 1982.**

Little Owly wants to know everything, and so he asks his mother to tell him how many stars there are in the sky, how many waves there are in the ocean, how high the sky is, how deep the ocean is. These wonderings may inspire students to pose some of their own big number questions, and then to research the answers.

Veltman, John. *Binary Power*. **Dale Seymour Publications, 1992.**

An excellent resource book for teachers that discusses geometric progression.

Wells, Robert. *Is a Blue Whale the Biggest Thing There Is?* **Albert Whitman, 1993.**

The message of this book is that the universe is a big place and so we need big numbers to describe it. The book tells about progressively larger things: blue whales, Mount Everest, the earth, the sun, stars, galaxies. It compares these gigantic things in imaginative ways. For example, 100 earths stuffed into a bag would not come close to the size of our sun. Students can use some of their own data to make other big number comparisons.

More about literature and mathematics—good reading for teachers!

Illingworth, Mark. *Real-Life Problem Solving*. **Scholastic Professional Books, 1996.**

Piccirilli, Richard. *Write About Math*. **Scholastic Professional Books, 1996.**

Whitin, David J. and Sandra Wilde. *It's the Story that Counts*. **Heinemann, 1995.**

_____. *Read Any Good Math Lately?* **Heinemann, 1992.**

Name _____ Date _____

What would I do with one million?

Think about a wish for a million of something.
Then complete the sentences below.
Be ready to share your ideas!

1. I wish I had 1,000,000 _____ .

2. I wouldn't want 1,000,000 _____ .

3. I can make 1,000,000 _____ .

4. I could eat 1,000,000 _____ .

5. I could never eat 1,000,000 _____ .

6. Having 1,000,000 _____ would be great!

7. Having 1,000,000 _____ could be a problem.

8. If I had $1,000,000 I would _____

_____

_____

_____

_____

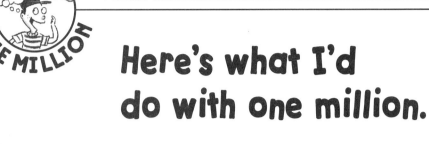

Name _____ Date _____

Here's what I'd do with one million.

Read the list of things you might have one million of.
Write what you would do with each.

If I had a million . . .   I would . . .

chances _____

books _____

friends _____

lives _____

pieces of clothing _____

dogs _____

fishing poles _____

cars _____

video games _____

wishes _____

jelly beans _____

brains _____

trees _____

Now make a list of your own.
Exchange your list with a friend and complete the list you receive.

If I had a million . . .   I would . . .

_____   _____

_____   _____

_____   _____

Name _____ Date _____

How long does it take to count to one million?

Follow the directions and record your findings.
Be ready to report to the class!

1. Use a clock or watch. As one person in your group counts aloud, time him or her for one minute. What number did the counter reach? _____

2. If that was the number your group reached in one minute, and all the numbers took the same amount of time to say, how high could you count in . . .

   a. ten minutes? _____   **c.** one day? _____

   b. one hour? _____   **d.** five days? _____

3. How long would it take to count to one million? How did you figure it out?

   _____

   _____

4. What things make a difference in how fast you can count numbers?

   _____

   _____

5. Compare your group's findings with other groups in your class. What do you discover? Complete the chart to show the results.

Time It Took to Count to One Million	
Group	Time

Name _____   Date _____

How does skip-counting make it faster to count to one million?

Use your data from your first investigation for the starting point—the time it took to count to one million by 1s. Assume all the numbers take the same amount of time to say. Then follow the directions below. Record your findings.

1. Pick another number to count by. It might be 5, 10, 100, or even 1,000. Write the number here. _____

2. Use a clock or watch with a second hand. As one person in your group counts, time him or her for one minute. How high did the person count? _____

3. If that was your number in one minute, how long would it take to count to one million? _____

4. Now make a chart of all the different numbers that groups in your class used to count by. Record the results. Do you see any patterns? For example, is counting by 10s twice as fast as counting by 5s? How many times faster is it to count by 10s than by 5s?

| Time It Took to Count to One Million ||
Number Counted By	Time

6. What interesting discoveries did you make when you counted by a number other than 1? Write one of your discoveries here.

_____

_____

_____

The Magic of a Million Activity Book Scholastic Professional Books

Name _____ Date _____

Is it faster to count aloud to one million or to write numbers from one to one million?

Write down the average number your class counters reached after one minute. Use this as your starting number. Figure out how long it would take to write numbers up to one million, if all the numbers took the same time to write.

1. Number reached in one minute:

_____

2. Time to reach one million:

_____

3. Here's how I got my answer: _____

_____

_____

_____

_____

4. I think my result is (accurate/not accurate) because _____

_____

_____

_____

_____

COUNTING TO ONE MILLION
1 2 3 ...

Name _____   Date _____

How long does it take to reach one million using doubling?

Use your weekly allowance as a way to investigate one million.

1. Start with your weekly allowance. If you don't get an allowance, pretend that it is $3.00 each week. How many weeks would it take for you to have at least $1,000,000? _____ weeks

2. Perhaps your parents would agree to a different monthly payment schedule. If you were paid 1 penny on the first day of the month, 2 pennies on the second day, 4 pennies on the third day, 8 pennies on the fourth day, and so on until the end of 30 days, would you be better off? Record the information on the chart. How much would you receive on the 30th day?

3. How much money would you have all together, if you were to add up everything you have received at the end of 30 days? (Hint: You can add all the amounts together—or look for a pattern by figuring out the total after the 3rd day, the 5th day, the 8th day.)

Day	I will have . . .	Day	I will have . . .
1	$0.01	16	
2	$0.02	17	
3	$0.04	18	
4	$0.08	19	
5		20	
6		21	
7		22	
8		23	
9		24	
10		25	
11		26	
12		27	
13		28	
14		29	
15		30	

_____

The Magic of a Million Activity Book Scholastic Professional Books

Name _____ Date _____

How can we keep track of one million things?

Follow these steps to help you collect and group one million.

1. With your class, decide what you will collect. Write the name of your item here. _____

2. Decide on an orderly way to count and store your things. For example, you might make groups of 100. Keep track of the following numbers on your way to one million.

   ★ 100 is _____ groups of 10.

   ★ 1,000 is _____ groups of 100, or _____ groups of 10.

   ★ 10,000 is _____ groups of 1,000, or _____ groups of 100.

   ★ 100,000 is _____ groups of 10,000, or _____ groups of 1,000, or _____ groups of 100.

   ★ 1,000,000 is _____ groups of 100,000, or _____ groups of 10,000, or _____ groups of 1,000.

3. Look at the number of zeros after the number 1 in each of the following numbers. Write down what you discover.

   1 [one] _____

   10 [ten] _____

   100 [one hundred] _____

   1,000 [one thousand] _____

   10,000 [ten thousand] _____

   100,000 [one hundred thousand] _____

   1,000,000 [one million] _____

Name _____ Date _____

How can we collect and keep track of a million pennies?

Make a thermometer graph like the one shown to record progress toward your goal as your class penny collection grows. Each week, record on the chart the number of pennies the class collects. Then, add that amount to the previous total to keep showing the new amount collected and the new total. Extend your chart with extra pieces of paper if you want to show more than 15 weeks.

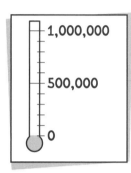

Week	Number of Pennies Collected	Cumulative Total
1		
2		
3		
4		
5		
6		
7		
8		
9		
10		
11		
12		
13		
14		
15		

Name _____ Date _____

What things from an assorted collection go together?

Use the chart to show some categories you could make from your classroom collection. Write the names of three categories. Then list things from the collection, and other things you can think of, that would belong in each category.

Category 1	Category 2	Category 3
Things that are _____	Things that are _____	Things that are _____
_____	_____	_____
_____	_____	_____
_____	_____	_____

Now put your items in the Venn diagram.
The center is for items that share all three attributes.

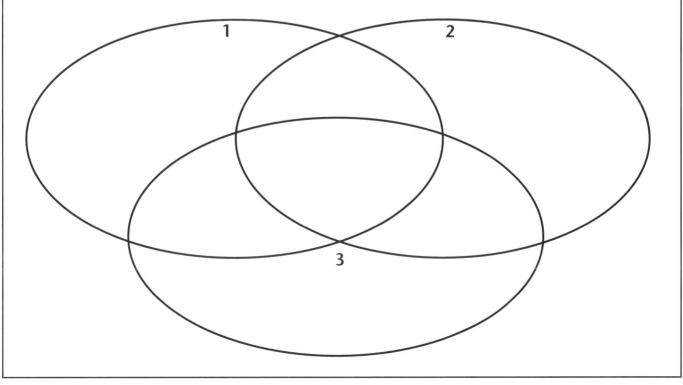

COLLECTING ONE MILLION

Name _____   Date _____

How many books would one million letters fill?

Fill in the information below. Be ready to report the information for your book.

1. Title of book: _____

2. Type of book: _____

3. Number of pages: _____

4. Number of books needed to make 1,000,000 pages:

   _____

5. Average number of words per page: _____

6. Number of pages needed to make 1,000,000 words:

   _____

7. Average number of letters per page: _____

8. Number of pages needed to make 1,000,000 letters:

   _____

9. Here are some other interesting facts I've discovered about books, pages, words, and letters:

   _____

   _____

   _____

   _____

   _____

   The Magic of a Million Activity Book Scholastic Professional Books

Name _____ Date _____

How can we create a mosaic mural of one million 1-cm squares?

Color a pattern on your grid. Put it together with others to make a Million Mosaic.

Name _____ Date _____

How can we put cubes together to make a million-cube?

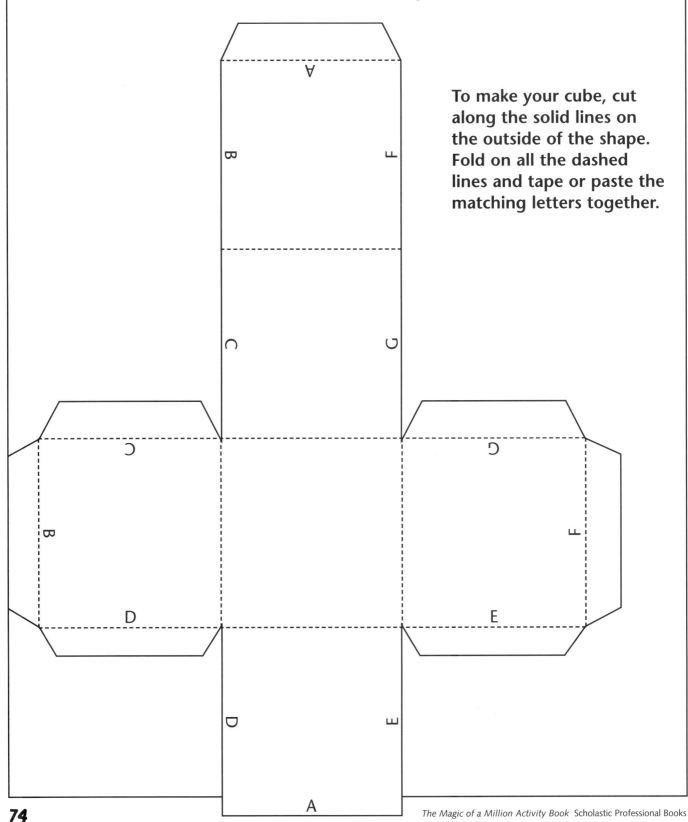

To make your cube, cut along the solid lines on the outside of the shape. Fold on all the dashed lines and tape or paste the matching letters together.

The Magic of a Million Activity Book Scholastic Professional Books

CALCULATING ONE MILLION

1,000,000

Name _____ Date _____

What do humans do a million or more times a year?

Record the problem you investigated and your findings.
Be ready to share them with the class!

What we investigated:

_____

_____

_____

_____

_____

Here are our calculations and results:

_____

_____

_____

_____

_____

_____

_____

Name _____   Date _____

Do we go to school for one million days?

Complete the following information about your school district

1. Number of days in the school year: _____

2. Number of years in elementary school: _____

3. Number of years in middle school or junior high school: _____

4. Number of years in high school: _____

5. Number of years I think I will go to college: _____

6. Total number of days I will spend in school: _____

7. I would have to go to school for _____ more days or

   _____ more years to go to school for one million days.

   I would graduate in the year _____.

The Magic of a Million Activity Book Scholastic Professional Books

Name _____ Date _____

How long would it take to watch one million hours of television?

1. Use the chart to record the number of hours you generally watch TV.

Hours of Daily TV	Average Number of Hours
Monday to Thursday	
Friday	
Saturday	
Sunday	

2. My weekly average is _____ hours, or _____ minutes, of TV.

3. If I watch _____ hours each week, it will take _____ weeks

or _____ years to watch one million hours of TV.

4. In each hour there are usually _____ minutes of commercials.

So here is the amount of time I watch commercials.

Minutes of Commercials Daily:

Monday to Thursday _____

Friday _____

Saturday _____

Sunday _____

CALCULATING ONE MILLION

1,000,000

Name _____   Date _____

How far is one million?

Figure out each distance. Write or show your
work to explain how you got your answers.

How many miles is . . .

1. One million inches?	2. One million feet?	3. One million yards?

How many kilometers is . . .

1. One million centimeters?	2. One million decimeters?	3. One million meters?

The Magic of a Million Activity Book Scholastic Professional Books

Name _____ Date _____

How long would it take to walk one million paces?

Complete the information below.
Be ready to share your findings!

1. The distance I used was: _____

2. The time it took me to walk that distance was: _____

3. At that rate, it would take this amount of time to walk one million paces:

   _____ minutes

   _____ hours

   _____ days

4. Here is more information I know about distances:

   _____

   _____

   _____

   _____

   _____

   _____

   _____

   _____

   _____

   _____

Name _____ Date _____

How can you use the newspaper to investigate one million?

Use a page of the newspaper to find the following information.

1. What kind of newspaper page did you use? For example, did you have a local news page? A sports page? An advertising page?

   _____

   _____

   _____

2. How many numbers did you find on your page? What were the numbers?

   _____

   _____

3. If that was the typical number of numbers on a newspaper page, how many pages long would the paper need to be to have one million numbers?

   _____

   _____

   _____

4. Here are my conclusions about numbers in the news:

   _____

   _____

   _____

   _____

   _____

The Magic of a Million Activity Book Scholastic Professional Books